A Special Issue of

Sponsored by the National Council on Compulsive Gambling, Inc.

COMPULSIVE GAMBLING

An Examination of Relevant Models

Edited by Julian I. Taber, Ph.D.

HUMAN SCIENCES PRESS, INC.
72 FIFTH AVENUE
NEW YORK, N.Y. 10011-8004   (212) 243-6000

RC 569.5
.G35
C66
1987

ISBN: 0-89885-392-3

Copyright 1987 by Human Sciences Press
72 Fifth Avenue
New York, New York 10011

All rights reserved. No part of this work may be reproduced or utilized in any form or by any means, electronic or mechanical, including photocopying, microfilm, and recording, or by any information storage and retrieval system, without prior permission from the publisher in writing.

Printed in the United States of America.

ISBN 0-89885-392-3

CONTENTS

Volume 3, Number 4   Winter, 1987

Articles

Compulsive Gambling: An Examination of Relevant Models	*Julian I. Taber*	219
Models of Gambling and Gambling Addictions as Perceptual Filters	*R.I.F. Brown*	224
Compulsive Gambling and the Medical Model	*Sheila B. Blume*	237
The Future of Gambling Research: Learning from the Lessons of Alcoholism	*Mark Dickerson*	248
Pathological Gambling: A Parsimonious Need State Model	*Richard A. McCormick*	257
Economic Perceptions of Gambling Behavior	*William R. Eadington*	264
Physiological Factors as Determinants of Pathological Gambling	*Peter L. Carlton* *Paul Manowitz*	274

Book Reviews

Compulsive Gamblers by Mark Dickerson	*Martin Chaplin*	286

The Chase by Henry Lesieur	Terry J. Knapp	288
Thinking Big by Sol Fox	Charles D. Maurer	291

Index   295

The **JOURNAL OF GAMBLING BEHAVIOR** is sponsored by the National Council on Compulsive Gambling, the only voluntary health agency established to combat the disease of pathological gambling. This quarterly journal is devoted to the understanding of gambling behavior and pathologic gambling. Professionals from all disciplines are invited to submit articles, including professionals in the fields of anthropology, sociology, economics, political science, criminology, psychology, social work, and psychiatry. Awareness and arousal of interest in gambling and pathological gambling and its treatment is the prime focus of this journal.

MANUSCRIPTS must be typed double-spaced on one side and submitted in triplicate (one original and two photocopies) to the Editor, Henry R. Lesieur, National Council on Compulsive Gambling, Inc., c/o John Jay College of Criminal Justice, 444 West 56th Street, Room 3207S, New York, NY 10019. References should be listed following the style of the American Psychological Association Publication Manual, 3rd Edition, 1983 Revision.

SUBSCRIPTIONS are on a calendar year basis: $88 for institutions and $34 for individuals. Membership in the National Council on Compulsive Gambling includes subscription to the journal. **ADVERTISING** rates are available on request. Advertising and subscription inquiries should be made to Human Sciences Press, 72 Fifth Avenue, New York, NY 10011. (212) 243-6000.

INDEXED OR ABSTRACTED IN: Sociological Abstracts & SOPODA, Chicago Psychoanalytic Literature Index, Human Resources Abstracts and APA Psychological Abstracts.

PHOTOCOPYING: Authorization to photocopy items for internal or personal use, or the internal use of specific clients, is granted by Human Sciences Press for users registered with the Copyright Clearance Center (CCC) Transitional Reporting Service, provided that the base fee of $2.50 per copy, plus $.20 per page is paid directly to CCC, 27 Congress St., Salem, MA 01970. For those organizations that have been granted a photocopy licence by CCC, a separate system of payment has been arranged. The fee code for users of the Transactional Reporting Service is: ISSN 0742-0714/87 $2.50 + .20.

COPYRIGHT 1987 by Human Sciences Press, Inc. Published quarterly in the Spring, Summer, Fall and Winter. Second-class postage pending at New York, NY and at additional mailing offices. **POSTMASTER:** Send change of address and return journal if undeliverable to Human Sciences Press, 72 Fifth Avenue, New York, NY 10011. Please return entire journal—do not remove cover.

ISSN 0742-0714
© 1987 Human Sciences Press

Compulsive Gambling: An Examination of Relevant Models

Julian I. Taber, Ph.D.
Chief, Addictive Disorders Treatment Program
Ioannis A. Lougaris Veterans Administration Medical Center
1000 Locust Street
Reno, Nevada 89520

In October of 1978, at the invitation of Gamblers Anonymous, I drove from Cleveland to Buffalo to be a guest at a weekend regional conclave of G.A. and Gam-Anon. With a full two weeks of experience in working with pathological gamblers behind me I was indeed an innocent entering the lion's pit. I lingered on at Brecksville, Ohio working with gamblers for another seven years, but no subsequent events impressed me more than this abrupt introduction to the people, stories and situations that are at once so painful and compelling.

All went well during the first day. Msgr. Joseph Dunne broke into the local jail and returned with two desperate gamblers whom I interviewed on the spot. There I sat in a deserted cocktail lounge hearing this poor man's story, tears streaming down his face, with a ventriloquist practicing his act in the background. I survived the formal dinner that night with only a near fatal heart palpitaion: after dinner, you see,

---

This paper was written to serve as a brief introduction to a collection of invited papers on models of pathological gambling. The author served as editor of the special edition of the Journal of Gambling Behavior in which these papers are to appear.

Send reprint requests to: Julian I. Taber, Ph.D. Chief, Addictive Disorders Treatment Program Ioannis A. Lougaris Veterans Administration Medical Center 1000 Locust Street Reno, Nevada 89520.

they took up a collection. Large silver trays were passed through the crowded hall, but being at the dais I was among the last to be solicited. As a man came lunging toward me with a huge tray piled high with bills I whispered to a G.A. man next to me, "How much should I give?"

"Double the pot," he answered.

Sunday morning. The chosen speaker, Ruth S., had to cancel. Taber is pressed into service as a visiting "expert."

Instead of giving a speech I modestly invited an open discussion. The first question, "Dr. Taber, do you think that compulsive gambling is a disease?"

The old habits of professorship took over and I launched into a learned and rambling discourse suggesting that statistical learning theory and schedules of reinforcement offered interesting insights. I soon sensed that something was causing considerable distress but no one was disrobing and I could not smell smoke. During a pause a man in the back stood up and instead of asking a question he asserted that the G.A. program had saved his life, that gambling was a disease and that by suggesting that it might not be a disease I was placing other lives in jeopardy. Others quickly began to press the disease model upon me; some were pleading and anxious, others were red-faced and angry.

I had not gone there to distress anyone and certainly had no wish to kill off compulsive gamblers with my opinions. As I learned there that Sunday, freedom of speech was not to be part of my interaction with self-help groups nor, in fact, were ideas really what they needed from me. In attending many other meetings and conclaves over the years I learned that they needed my ears much more than my tongue, and they taught me to take much satisfaction in making that offering. But, now, in this special issue, I have at last found a forum, one respected in both self-help and professional circles, for some of the best minds in the field to express their widely differing and, yes, often upsetting ideas.

The intellectual needs of scientists and practitioners are legitimately different from the needs of those they serve and most certainly should not be limited uncritically, either through laziness or unseemly deference, to those allowed us by our clients. To invest in any single formula would constitute irrational, long-shot gambling on our part since; no matter how useful and internally consistent any single model may be, none yet presented comes anywhere close to covering all human risk-taking situations.

JULIAN I. TABER

Problem, excessive and pathological gambling can be conceptualized in terms of addictionology, biology, genetics, disease process, values clarification, forensic responsibility, learning failure, developmental disorder, anthropological matrix, social dynamic, impulse control, economic man, political resource theory and, yes, in terms of statistical learning theory and schedules of reinforcement. To say that I need be concerned with only one or two of these models is to bet the long shot and risk it all, my own ego as well as the health prospects of the mental health services consumership.

Mere technicians are taught to adhere to a single model for they are not supposed to be able to think. Thus, they risk instant obsolescence when models change. If we adopt a "single cause" mentality with regard to gambling problems, or if we limit our concern to some small sub-sample of gamblers, we place at risk our academic and intellectual heritages. We risk becoming phobic of all possible competitors to our own theory. And, of course, we chance the strong probability that by exercising selective perception we will ignore or even harm others with legitimate interests and problems. We risk tolerating in ourselves a kind of dysphoric perceptual extremism that divides the world into black and white.

There is no argument here against specialization for it is through specialization that we become truly expert; the argument is that we should control technical specialization as we control any good tool, setting it aside from time to time in order to refresh intellect. We need not allow our world view to become subservient to familiar technologies or influenced by the worldly status and wealth that technical success brings.

Through the tolerance and hard work of the authors here present we have assembled what I hope may be the beginnings of a continuing dialogue between scholars in the field of risk-taking. In arranging for some of the leading figures in our field to present their personal views and theoretical models it was my hope that we would establish a model for future dialogues. It would be a serious error for the reader to assume that we are here staging a debate from which ultimately will emerge the one, the final, the really correct explanation of problem gambling. If we are to explain complex behavior we must learn to tolerate theoretical complexity: the history of science tells us that the more diverse the data base the more profound will be the grandeur and scope of our ultimate and inevitable simplifying assumptions.

The reader finds assembled here a distinguished panel of experts in the field of pathological gambling that is both international and multidisciplinary in composition. Each argues his or her views with vigor and with willingness to risk being wrong or incomplete in order to articulate a position with precision. Unsettling as it may seem, it is entirely possible for equally qualified scholars to be correct while holding what may seem to be opposing views. Is it a mark of my own intellectual weakness that I find myself persuaded equally by all the writers whose work is here included? I hope not.

I have chosen the work of R.I.F. Brown, an academic psychologist from Glasgow, to set the stage for this issue. Dr. Brown puts forth the case of social learning theory, but most importantly reminds us that theoretical models act as perceptual lenses that sometimes clarify and sometimes limit our vision. Next, the distinguished psychiatrist Sheila B. Blume articulates the essentials of the medical model that dominates thinking about problem gambling in the United States, a model that has revolutionized both treatment techniques and treatment funding. Next, Mark Dickerson, a psychologist from Australia whose book is reviewed by Martin Chaplin in this issue, shakes the foundations of the medical model by questioning its most basic assumptions. Dr. Dickerson, in fact, predicts an early demise of efforts to medicalize problem gambling.

Richard A. McCormick, whose continuing research at the Cleveland Veterans Administration Medical Center carries on that Center's tradition of work with pathological gamblers, offers a psychologist's relatively uncomplicated model of Directive State Theory; dominant emotional needs are seen as critical in the etiology of problem gambling. The career of the economist William R. Eadington has exemplified an enduring and distinguished contribution; he has done as much over the years as any other individual to bring together practitioners and scholars interested in problem gambling. Dr. Eadington reminds us that pathological gambling can never really be extracted from its economic matrix and that it can, in fact, be productively conceptualized as an economic phenomenon. One of the most intriguing papers is saved for last: Peter L. Carlton and Paul Manowitz are psychologists working in a department of psychiatry. They present convincing evidence that gambling and other addictions have some relationship to altered brain biochemistry and function.

JULIAN I. TABER

This issue, then, succeeds in bringing to our readership explicit formulations of at least a few of the dominant theoretical models of problem gambling: medical, social learning, directive state, economic, and biological. There are many other views and many other specialties yet to be heard from.

Models of Gambling and Gambling Addictions as Perceptual Filters

R.I F. Brown
Department of Psychology, University of Glasgow

Models, in the sense of loosely entertained clusters of beliefs, attitudes, assumptions and expectations which direct the work of researchers and clinicians, also act as perceptual filters, tending to focus the attention of those who use them on certain aspects of reality and relegating to the background or ignoring altogether other aspects of the field of study and action. The central characteristics of social learning and of medical models are briefly reviewed and they are compared as perceptual filters for their distorting effects on research in gambling and in gambling addictions and on intervention strategies for problem gamblers. It is concluded that the exclusive predominance of any one model leads to the impoverishment of both research and intervention.

Two of the major functions of theory are as a *tool* to provide a guide for research and treatment, and ultimately as a *goal* which summarizes the state of our knowledge in a particular field of study (Marx, 1963). But additionally, theories have a crucial primary function in providing us with a system for filtering out the confusing onrush of irrelevant observations, features and events. They help us organize meaning out of the whole and they allow us to attend only to as much information as we can process at the one time without becoming overwhelmed.

Send reprint requests to: R.I.F. Brown, Department of Psychology, Adam Smith Building, University of Glasgow, Glasgow G12 8RT, United Kingdom.

It is this function as a *perceptual filter* which sometimes directs our attention to details we might otherwise miss, as when the successful search for the planet Pluto was directed by a combination of Newtonian physics and the theory of relativity. At other times, theory as a perceptual filter can halt our progress for long periods because it directs our attention away from crucial information. People had been looking at genes and chromosomes down microscopes for more than a hundred years before Mendel's genetic theory became accepted and it was thought that there ought to be such entities and suddenly they were "seen" (Boring, 1950). Kuhn (1970) has clarified how paradigm shifts in science occur mainly through the *imperfect* workings of the perceptual filters because it is often mainly through the accumulation of observations which *do not* fit the theory, that the pressure for a change in perspective builds up.

If the widest possible base in observations and data is not used from the earliest stages in the construction of our theories, our perceptual filters will prove an obstacle to recognizing the importance and perhaps even the existence of significant areas of the total domain of study. It is just this problem which the dominance of the medical model inevitably exacerbates.

Strictly speaking the use of the term "model" is not justified in so far as it may imply a detailed and articulated explanation of the interaction of a definable group of component variables through a series of developmental stages. Rather we are here speaking of a paradigm shared by a philosophical school of several individual scholars, clinicians and researchers who tend to entertain a loosely unified cluster of beliefs, attitudes, assumptions and expectations which direct their work. Nevertheless "model" is a useful shorthand which has gained extensive use for such a paradigm.

SOME VARIETIES OF MEDICAL MODEL

Just as there are several different medical models of alcoholism (Heather and Robertson, 1985) so too it is necessary to recognize that there is not one but several forms of the medical model of "compulsive" gambling and each of these can be held in a sophisticated form or in a crude and debased form.

Gambling as a pre-existent physical abnormality. This often takes the form of a claim for an underlying genetic predisposition, the equivalent for gambling of the Alcoholics Anonymous claim for an allergy to alcohol. No research on the genetics of gambling has been published of equivalent status to Goodwin's (1976) or Shields' (1977) research on the genetics of alcoholism, but an interesting parallel can be found in Jacobs' (1986) description of one of the two necessary predisposing factors for the existence of the addictive personality syndrome. This is described as "a unipolar physiological resting state which is either chronically depressed or excited" or a "lifelong persistent state of either hypo- or hyper-arousal." Although Jacobs does not directly say so, the implication seems to be that this is inherited in contrast to the psychological predisposing factors to the addictive personality syndrome which are clearly labelled as "arising from social and developmental experiences."

Gambling as a mental illness. Some subvarieties of this kind of medical model include seeing gambling as (a) an obsession (Reik, 1942; Leung, 1978); (b) a compulsion with a behavior completion mechanism (McConaghy, 1980; Leary and Dickerson, 1985); (c) a compulsion (Gamblers Anonymous) with loss of control in the same sense as a "disorder of impulse control" (American Psychiatric Association, 1980); or (d) a psychodynamic disorder (Freud, 1950; Bergler, 1957; Rosenthal, 1985).

Gambling as an acquired addiction or dependence. There seem to be no theories which are the equivalent for gambling of the alcohol dependence syndrome (Edwards and Gross, 1977; Edwards, 1986) in that they see gambling as a learned dependence with a predominantly physical basis. The nearest approach to that position is in those theories stressing the importance of an arousal component (Brown, 1986; Blasczynski, Winter and McConaghy, 1986; Dickerson and Adcock, 1987), but while many or most of these see problem gambling as an acquired addiction, most would *not* see addictions as illnesses and none see their models as in any sense "medical," nor do they put such central importance as Edward's alcohol dependence syndrome on physical dependence defined as "tolerance, withdrawal symptoms, relief drinking, and reinstatement."

R.I.F. BROWN

COGNITIVE SOCIAL LEARNING MODELS

Social learning models as applied to the addictions are derived ultimately from psychological theories of learning and personality with much wider applications (Mischel, 1973; Bandura, 1977, Rotter et al., 1972). The most thorough and comprehensive attempt to apply an explicitly social learning perspective to the construction of a developmental and analytical account of all addictions is that of Orford (1985). He makes a detailed analysis of features common to all addictions and follows them through several developmental stages using nothing more than the systems of psychological explanation developed for the study of everyday "normal" phenomena. There have been several attempts to construct social learning theories of alcoholism (Plant, 1979; Heather and Robertson, 1985 and Marlatt, 1985).

Although many partial theories of gambling are implicitly within a social learning framework, (e.g. Dickerson and Adcock, 1987; Blasczynski, Winter and McConaghy, 1986), no attempt has been made to construct a fully comprehensive explanation of gambling within an explicitly social learning theory framework. Nevertheless, Cornish (1978), Dickerson (1984) and Brown (1986), all of whom have made broad reviews of gambling with varying thoroughness, all appear to work within a predominantly (but not exclusively) social learning paradigm.

A social learning theory of gambling which followed similar theories of drinking and illegal drug abuse would probably suggest that gambling begins with imitation learning, perhaps copying a hero figure in adolescence, but more commonly learning from one's social peers. The ensuing frequency of gambling and amounts gambled are affected by the social context of the gambler, especially by the opportunities afforded by one's occupation, the leisure habits and facilities of one's neighborhood, the habits of peers and by several features of lifestyle, such as use of money. Once gambling becomes frequent enough to begin to have an adaptational function for the individual, usually in arousal stimulation and/or escape, major losses occur and chasing them begins. The individual then develops several new strategies for raising money with which to gamble. Successive life crises, latterly brought on by the gambling itself, each tend to lead to increases in gambling followed by plateaux. Finally gambling is associated with complex cues (times, people, places, events, situations) which may sensitize the gambler to expect to gamble and each gambling episode set off in this way tends to lead to prolonged attempts to chase losses which in turn lead to still greater losses.

Social learning theories of gambling and other addictions are as varied in their mix of components and balance of emphases as are the disease process theories discussed earlier, but they tend to have the following components in common:

1. It is expected that the one general scheme of explanation will be applicable to a spectrum of addictions, e.g. to heroin, sex, alcohol, caffeine, etc., of which gambling is only one.
2. It is expected that problem gambling will not be found to be a single unified phenomenon with a sharp cutoff point from all other forms of gambling but will rather be found to be a part of a statistical continuum of distribution from problem free to problem dominated gambling. Even at the problem dominated end of the continuum, there will be found to be several subtypes of problem gamblers, e.g., possibly associated with manic depressive (McCormick, Russo, Ramirez, and Taber, 1984) or psychopathic disorders, with subcultural differences, or with individual escapist or sensation seeking needs (Anderson and Brown, 1984, Blasczynski, Wilson and McConaghy, 1985), etc.
3. It is expected that one general scheme of explanation will be applicable to the whole range of phenomena, from normal (problem-free) gambling through several "grey areas" of heavy gambling and problem gambling to the most extreme instances of addicted gambling attended by the most acute and comprehensive range of problems.
4. It is recognized that systems of self-monitoring, self-control and self-evaluation which commonly hold normal gambling behavior in check (Premack, 1970; Kanfer and Karoly, 1972) are still present and operative even in the most extreme addicted gambler who is never completely out of control all the time although control may be patchy and impaired at frequent intervals.
5. It is expected that the course of development of individual gambling problems, although frequently conforming to a discernible pattern, is not a uniform, far less an inexorable progression. Many individuals are expected to move into and out of

gambling problems several times in the course of a life career in gambling (Stimson, Oppenheimer and Thorley, 1978).
6. It is expected that a comprehensive explanation in social learning terms will call upon a wide variety of already well known psychological phenomena and will have interfaces with and be compatible with several disciplines operating at different levels of explanation, both molar and molecular, e.g., with sociological (Abt, McGurrin and Smith, 1986), physiological (Brown, 1986; Jacobs, 1986) and genetic (Goodwin, 1976) components in a general model.
7. It is expected that problem gambling as predominantly a learned phenomenon, can be unlearned, at least in theory, implying that even some of the most severe gambling problems need not be irreversible and that total abstinence from gambling is not the only possible treatment goal (Dickerson and Weeks, 1979; McConaghy, Armstrong, Blaszczynski and Allcock, 1983; Brown, 1987b, in press).
8. It is recognized that treatment by professional skills or through self help groups is not always necessary for recovery and that many individuals with severe problems recover on their own (McPeek, 1972; Russell, 1973).
9. It is recognized that, as part of a wider society and culture which has a recognizable influence on their behavior, individual gamblers are affected by social and legal controls and policies and that such social policies may have an important role to play in the control of gambling problems (Heather and Robertson, 1985).

OVERLAP BETWEEN SOCIAL LEARNING AND MEDICAL MODELS

Social learning theory can easily integrate some forms of the "Preexisting Physical Abnormality" variety of the medical model—inherited differences in arousal (Jacobs, 1986), for example—but tend to reject outright the various sub-varieties of the "Gambling as Mental Illness" variety.

Thus the "Gambling as an obsession" sub-variety may be rejected on the basis of the poor support that empirical tests of it appear to bring (Leung, 1978; Leary and Dickerson, 1985). Similarly it is difficult to uphold a conception of gambling as a "disorder of impulse control" when there is daily clinical evidence that many individual "compulsive" gamblers promise themselves reversions, relapses "slips" or "falls," build up to them over a long period in advance, sometimes plan them out carefully and then execute the plan with decision, flexibility and efficiency. This may be thought to be a very strange "impulse" indeed, and the clinical evidence is backed up by research evidence (O'Donnell, 1984) and can be accounted for by a learning theory based, affective decision-making, theoretical explanation of such apparently deliberate and planned "impulses" (Brown, 1987a, *in press*).

Social learning theorists commonly use the term "addiction" and, since this is a term also used in the "Gambling as Acquired Addiction or Dependence" variety of medical model, this might be construed as at least one overlap with the medical model, if not an acceptance. But that would be quite illusory because most social learning oriented researchers do not see that addictions are illnesses at all and several attempts have been made to demonstrate that addictions can be explained much better without recourse to any of the illness concepts (Orford, 1985; Heather and Robertson, 1985).

MEDICAL MODELS AND SOCIAL LEARNING MODELS COMPARED AS A PERCEPTUAL FILTERS

Both models, whether held in relatively sophisticated and flexible or in crude and rigid forms, have some major distorting effects on our perceptions of all gambling, and on our intervention strategies for problem gambling.

Deficiencies of the medical model as a Guide to Research. The focus of concern in a medical model is inevitably on the sick and frequently on the sickest. This means that the sample of gamblers studied is almost exclusively those who are present at treatment agencies and little or nothing is known (and few questions are asked) about the others, probably the majority of gamblers, who (a) have acute and intractable problems and never present for treatment, (b) have acute problems and overcome them themselves or without the aid of conventional treatment, (c) gamble heavily from time to time but with intermediate levels of problems, (d) gamble without more than passing light problems, (e) gamble with unremitting pleasure or even profit. Although these last five categories together appear to make up the vast majority of gamblers, a virtue is often made of studying even the few most extreme cases among the obviously sick sample on the grounds that it may be among the most extreme that the characteristics of the pathological gambler can most clearly be seen and the processes of the illness are most likely to be identified. The contrast between the narrow focus of the medical model and the broad interests of the social learning model in a continuum of problems of varying severity is obvious.

An illness analogy in its cruder forms assume a simple dichotomy between the "sick" gambler on the one hand and the "normal" gambler on the other and a sizeable qualitative gap between normal and pathological. This leads to failure to recognize the more important similarities between the two. For example, the pathological gambler is seen as subject to an irresistible compulsion process, which results in comprehensive or even total loss of control, while on the other hand the "normal" gambler is seen as exercising free will, ignoring the elements of praxis in the first and of process in the second.

The cruder forms of illness analogy may also lead us to expect that pathological gambling will be a unity and that the disease processes will be similar in all pathological gamblers, thus directing attention away from the demonstrable existence of sub-types of problem gambler.

In a laudable effort to educate the public away from the moral model with its implications of responsibility for actions and attendant punishments, the medical model has devalued the real importance of decision-making in the development, maintenance and recovery from gambling problems compared with the central position given to it in the moral model and the important role assigned to it in social learning models (Orford, 1985).

The tendency of a medical model of other addictions to lead to a concentration on physical factors in explanation has been much less evident with gambling, partly because it has been, until recently, relatively more difficult to find a physical basis for the behavior when no substance is ingested.

Deficiencies of a Social Learning Model as a Guide to Research. In common with all behavioral theories of learning from which it is derived, the social learning model tends to underestimate the importance of internal events, such as perception, emotion and thinking. The genetics of gambling have received no attention at all, even from proponents of the medical model.

In contrast to the typical behaviorist neglect of emotions in general and of arousal as linked to them, many students of gambling and gambling problems have commented on the apparently central importance of arousal and elation in gambling and, more recently, some researchers and theorists have begun to incorporate the phenomenon as a major or even a central component in their theories (Anderson and Brown, 1984, 1987; Leary and Dickerson, 1985; Blaszczynski, Winter and McConaghy, 1986; Jacobs, 1986).

Similarly, in contrast to the traditional behaviorist denial of the relevance of phenomenology or self-reported personal experience, work is beginning on a structured phenomenology of addictions (including gambling) which links easily with learning theory formulations (Anderson and Brown, 1987; Brown, 1987a, in press, 1987b, in press).

In terms of Alexander and Hadaway's distinction between two broad classes of theories of addiction as "exposure" theories and "adaptation" theories (Alexander and Hadaway, 1982), most social learning theorists place much more emphasis on the effects of exposure to external social influences as causal factors in the development and maintenance of the addictions. This can lead to the relative neglect of the adaptive function that the learned addictive activity can play for each individual as a form of self medication for current emotional and social problems.

Deficiencies of the Medical Model as a Guide to Treatment. Because illness models tend to focus on the sick, they naturally tend to lead to treatment methods which are appropriate only for the sick and sometimes only for the most seriously sick. In the addictions field this has meant in the past an almost exclusive focus on total abstinence programs of treatment. These methods are often inappropriate for the heavy or early stage user who may do best with one of the innovative treatment methods generated, by proponents of social learning theory (Miller and Munoz, 1976; Dickerson and Weeks, 1979; Rankin, 1981; Greenberg and Rankin, 1982; McConaghy, Armstrong, Blaszcynski and Allcock, 1983;

Heather, Whitton and Robertson, 1986; Brown, 1987b). Illness models tend to take the focus of attention away from preventative measures which are likely to be effective with the larger majority of the population of frequent and infrequent users who are not identifiable as abusers but which will contain many potential abusers who could be arrested at an earlier stage.

The use of disease models usually involves a labelling process which leads to a change in self identity on the part of the "sick," leading to a lifelong career of separateness from the rest of the community or to a career in deviance. Others then coming to these groups with identities apart, resist the transition to membership of what they see as a deviant group, and hence delay seeking treatment (Sagarin, 1969).

Because the medical model is so familiar in other settings such as the treatment of physical disease, it appears to assume not only a disease process over which the sufferer has little or no control, but also to suggest that the responsibility for change and recovery is not that of the "sufferer" but rather that of the "expert" who will actively treat a relatively passive "patient." This has the effect, in contrast with the assumptions of the social learning model, of elevating "expert" help (perhaps including even self-help groups) out of all proportion to its real use, especially with the problems of the larger group of mere "heavy users" as opposed to "real addicts" (Orford, 1985).

Therefore the medical models lead to a group of unacceptably narrow theories based upon very small samples of the total domain of the phenomenon studied which in turn gravely limit the types of intervention available.

Deficiencies of the Social Learning Model as a Guide to Treatment. The social learning theory model tends to produce complex and detailed explanations and has no familiar analogy in everyday life which is easily understood by the layman. By contrast the medical model of pathological gambling produces in the "illness" or "disease" analogy a framework for understanding and changing the attitudes of gambler and family to problems which can be understood and applied more immediately and easily by the layman coming to the problem for the first time. This is an advantage in the early stages of treatment in promoting a change in gambling behavior. But as the individual gambler successfully maintains a program of recovery, the very simplicity of the illness analogy, and especially of some of the assumptions that usually go with it, can become hindrances in reaching the full potential of the individual for recovery and reintegration within the community.

The innovative intervention strategies often generated by the social learning model are all too often first expressed in forbiddingly technical language and do not appear to be accessible to the ordinary layman to apply successfully to oneself and in self-help groups to others. This difficulty can usually be overcome, as several successful self-help books (Miller and Munoz, 1976; Robertson and Heather, 1986) and prevention studies using them (Heather, Whitton and Robertson, 1986) have demonstrated in the alcohol field, but, for the great majority of those seeking help, the illness analogy is still more immediately understandable amidst their panic and confusion.

CONCLUSION

Even if the social learning theory paradigm were to become dominant, the medical, moral and other perspectives on gambling and problem gambling will always remain important and sometimes useful alternative ways of viewing gambling phenomena. The exclusive, or even predominant, use of only one theoretical model tends to imply it's abuse as an involuntary perceptual filter and inevitably leads to distorted views of gambling and so to the impoverishment of both research an intervention.

REFERENCES

Abt, V., McGurrin, M.C. and Smith, J.F. (1986). Towards a synoptic model of gambling behavior. *Journal of Gambling Behavior, 1,* 79–88.
Alexander, B., and Hadaway, P. (1982). Opiate addiction: The case for an adaptive orientation. *Psychological Bulletin, 92,* 367–381.
American Psychiatric Association, (1980). *Diagnostic and Statistical Manual of Mental Disorders, (3rd ed.).* Washington, D.C.; American Psychiatric Association.
Anderson, G. & Brown, R.I.F. (1984). Real and laboratory gambling, sensation seeking and arousal. *British Journal of Psychology, 75,* 401–410.
Anderson, G. & Brown, R.I.F. (1987). Some applications of reversal theory to the explanation of gambling and gambling addictions. *Journal of Gambling Behavior, 3,*179–189.
Bandura, A. (1977). *Social learning theory.* Prentice-Hall: Englewood Cliffs, New Jersey.
Bergler, E. (1957). *The psychology of gambling.* Hill and Wang: New York.

Blasczynski, A., Wilson, A.C. and McConaghy, N. (1985). Sensation seeking and pathological gambling. *British Journal of Addiction, 81,* 113-117.
Blasczynski, A., Winter, S.W. and McConaghy, N. (1986). Plasma endorphin levels in pathological gambling. *Journal of Gambling Behavior, 2,* 3-14.
Boring, E.G. (1950). *History of experimental psychology.* Appleton-Century-Crofts: New York.
Brown, R.I.F. (1986). Arousal and sensation seeking components in the general explanation of gambling and gambling addictions. *International Journal of Addictions, 21,* 1001-1016.
Brown, R.I.F. (1987a). Gambling addictions, arousal and an affective decision making explanation of relapse. *International Journal of Addictions.* (in press).
Brown, R.I.F. (1987b). Classical and Operant Paradigms in the Management of Gambling Addictions. *Behavioural Psychotherapy, 15,* 111-122.
Cornish, D.B. (1978). *Gambling: A review of the literature and its implications for policy and research.* Her Majestie's Stationery Office, Home Office Research Study No. 42: London.
Dickerson, M.R. (1984). *Compulsive Gamblers.* Longmans: Sydney.
Dickerson, M.R. and Adcock, S. (1987). Mood, arousal and cognitions in persistent gambling: Preliminary investigation of a theoretical model. *Journal of Gambling Behaviour, 1,* 3-15.
Dickerson, M.G. and Weeks, D. (1979). Controlled Gambling as a Therapeutic Technique for Compulsive Gamblers, *Journal Behaviour Therapy and Experimental Psychiatry, 10,* 139-141.
Edwards, G. (1986). The alcohol dependency syndrome: a concept as stimulus to enquiry. *British Journal of Addiction, 81,* 171-193.
Edwards, G. and Gross, M. (1976). Alcohol dependence: Provisional description of a clinical syndrome. *British Medical Journal, i,* 1058-1061.
Freud, S. (1950). Dostoevsky and parricide. In *Collected Works.* Hogarth Press (originally 1929): London.
Goodwin, D. (1976). *Is alcoholism hereditary?* Oxford University Press: New York.
Greenberg, D. and Rankin, H. (1982). Compulsive Gamblers in Treatment. *British Journal Psychiatry, 140,* 364-366.
Heather, N. and Robertson, I. (1985). *Problem drinking: The new approach.* Penguin: Harmondsworth.
Heather, N., Whitton, B. and Robertson, I. (1986). Evaluation of a self help manual for media-recruited problem drinkers: Six-month follow-up results. *British Journal of Clinical Psychology, 25,* 19-34.
Jacobs, D. (1986). A general theory of addictions: A new theoretical model. *Journal of Gambling Behavior, 2,* 15-31.
Kanfer, F. and Karoly, P. (1972). Self control: A behavioristic excursion into the lion's den. *Behavior Therapy, 3,* 389-433.
Kuhn, T.S. (1970). *The structure of scientific revolutions.* (revised edition) University of Chicago Press: Chicago.
Leary, K. and Dickerson, M.R. (1985). Levels of arousal in high- and low-frequency gamblers. *Behaviour Research and Therapy, 17,* 459-466.
Leung, G.M.K.H. (1978). *A comparison of personalities of compulsive gamblers and obsessive-compulsive neurotics.* Unpublished M.Sc. thesis, University of Exeter; Exeter.
Marlatt, G.A. (1985). Relapse prevention: Theoretical rationale and overview of the model. In Marlatt, A.G. and Gordon, J.R. (eds), *Relapse prevention: Maintenance strategies in the treatment of addictive disorders.* Guildford Press: New York.
Marx, M.H. (1963). *Theories in Contemporary Psychology.* Macmillan: New York.
McConaghy, N. (1980). Behavior completion mechanisms rather than primary drives maintain behavioral patterns. *Activas Nervosa Superior* (Praha), *22,* 138-151.
McConaghy, N., Armstrong, M.S., Blasczynski, A. and Allcock, C. (1980). Controlled comparison of aversive and imaginal desensitization in compulsive gambling. *British Journal of Psychiatry, 142,* 366-372.
McCormick, R.A., Russo, A.M., Ramirez, L.F. and Taber, J.I. (1984). Affective disorders among pathological gamblers seeking treatment. *American Journal of Psychiatry, 141,* 215-218.
McPeek, F. (1972). The role of religious bodies in the treatment of alcohol in the United States. In *Alcohol, Science and Society: 29 Lectures with Discussions as Given at the Yale Summer School of Alcohol Studies.* Greenwood Press: Westport, Connecticut.

Miller, W. and Munoz, R. (1976). *How to control your drinking.* Prentice-Hall: Englewood Cliffs, New Jersey.
Mischell, W. (1973). Towards a cognitive social learning reconceptualization of personality. *Psychological Review, 80,* 252-283.
O'Donnell, P.J. (1984). The abstinence violation effect and circumstances surrounding relapse as predictors of outcome status in male alcoholic patients. *Journal of Psychology, 117,* 257-262.
Orford, J. (1985). *Excessive appetites: A psychological view of addictions.* Wiley: Chichester.
Plant, M.A. (1979). Learning to Drink. In Grant, M. and Gwinner, P. (Eds.) *Alcoholism in perspesctive.* Croom Helm: London.
Premack, D. (1970). Mechanisms of self control. In Hunt, W. (Ed.) *Learning Mechanisms in Smoking.* Aldine: Chicago.
Rankin, H. (1981). Control Rather than Abstinence as a Goal in the Treatment of Excessive Gambling. *Behaviour Research and Therapy, 20,* 185-187.
Reik, T. (1942). The study on Dostoevsky. In *Thirty years with Freud.* Hogarth Press: London.
Robertson, I. and Heather, N. (1986). *So you want to cut down your drinking?* British Psychological Society: Leicester.
Rosenthal, R.J. (1985). The pathological gambler's system for self-deception. In W.R. Eadington, *The Gambling Studies: Proceedings of the Sixth National Conference on Gambling and Risk Taking (vol. 5).* University of Nevada, Reno.
Rotter, J.B., Chance, J.E. and Phares, E.J. (eds.) (1972). *Some applications of a social learning theory of personality.* Holt, Rinehart and Winston: New York.
Russell, M. (1973). Changes in Cigarette Price and Consumption by Men in Britain, 1946-1971: A preliminary analysis. *British Journal of Preventative and Social Medicine, 27,* 1-7.
Sagarin, E. (1969). *Odd man in: Societies of deviants in America.* Quadrangle: Chicago.
Shields, J. (1977). Genetics and Alcoholism. In Edwards, G. & Grant, M. (eds.) *Alcoholism: New knowledge and new responses.* Croom Helm: London.
Stimson, G., Oppenheimer, E. and Thorley, A. (1978). Seven year follow-up of heroin addicts: Drug use and outcome. *British Medical Journal, i,* 1190-1192.

Compulsive Gambling and the Medical Model

Sheila B. Blume, M.D.
South Oaks Hospital, Amityville, New York

The medical model as a conceptual and operative approach to compulsive gambling is discussed. The terms "medical model" and "disease" are defined and the practical implications of their application to compulsive gambling are explored. Special attention is given to the "addictive disease" concept. Finally, a variety of objections to the medical model are described, but it is concluded that the many individual and social advantages of the medical model make it the preferred conceptualization at our present state of knowledge.

I DEFINITION

Considering the present state of our development, almost any concept of compulsive gambling one might choose to advance is likely to be controversial. Before embarking on a discussion of medical models, therefore, we must establish some definitions, lest we find ourselves like Alice in "Through the Looking Glass," debating with the famous philologist Humpty Dumpty:

> "When I use a word," Humpty Dumpty said, in a rather scornful tone, "it means just what I chose it to mean neither more nor less."

Send reprint requests to: Sheila B. Blume, M.D., Alcoholism and Compulsive Gambling Programs, South Oaks Hospital, 400 Sunrise Highway, Amityville, N.Y. 11701.

> "The question is," said Alice, "whether you can make words mean so many different things."
> "The question is," said Humpty Dumpty, "which is to be the master, that is all."

The term "medical model" means different things to different authors. Conrad and Schneider, in their volume *Deviance and Medicalization: From Badness to Sickness* (1980) point out that deviant behaviors can become redefined as medical conditions or "diseases" through a social and political process. They define "medical model" as follows:

> In this book we adopt a broad and pragmatic definition: the medical model of deviance locates the source of deviant behavior within the individual, postulating a physiological, constitutional, organic, or, occasionally, psychogenic agent or condition that is assumed to cause the behavioral deviance. The medical model of deviance usually, although not always, mandates intervention by medical personnel with medical means as treatment for the "illness" (Conrad and Schneider, 1980, p. 35).

I can accept this definition with one modification. Many diseases or pathological conditions are the result of the *interaction* between the human organism and the environment, rather than due to the action of internal factors alone. Examples are not hard to find. A small child falls into a swimming pool and is resuscitated, although not before anoxia has caused damage to her brain. The chronic stress of an air traffic controller's job interacts with physiological factors to produce a peptic ulcer, which heals when he changes jobs and recurs when he returns to the scope. A judge has an asthma attack when she enters a room where a cat has recently slept. Such examples are common in physical medicine. In the field of behavioral or mental disorder, interaction between individual and environment is the rule, rather than the exception. Even Alzheimer's disease, a physical deterioration of brain cells, will cause different manifestations in different people, in response to environmental variables.

II WHAT IS THE MEDICAL MODEL? WHAT IS IT NOT?

Since the medical model, when applied to a problem of behavior always subsumes a "disease" or "illness" concept of that behavior, a few words are in order about what the "disease concept" and "medical model" do and do not imply.

The medical model does *not* mean that *only* doctors treat an illness. Any one of a number of helping professions or an interdisciplinary team may be involved. It does not mean that the person with the illness, who assumes the "sick role," as described by Talcott Parsons (1951) and others, adopts a passive attitude (lying supine in bed if possible) while other people take responsibility for his/her life. One element of the sick role is the expectation that the individual wants to get well and seeks competent help (Parsons, 1951).

The "disease concept" does not imply that every disease is like smallpox, with a clearly defined single pathogen (a virus in this case) which attacks people more or less at random, by contagion, regardless of previous states of health. Multifactorial biopsychosocial models are more prevalent in psychiatry than single causation.

The word "disease" in this paper is used in its general English meaning, that is, a condition in which bodily health is seriously attacked, deranged, or impaired; sickness; illness (Webster, 1966). It is also, for this purpose, synonymous with the word "syndrome" (from the Greek "to run together"): "a group of signs and symptoms which occur together and characterize a disease" (Webster, 1966). In medicine the word syndrome is often used when the underlying pathogenesis of a condition is incompletely understood, and there may turn out to be more than one cause (e.g., nephrotic syndrome). The disease concept implies that one can say that individual A is suffering from an illness, that individual B is not, and individual C, showing some of the symptoms and signs but not others, is a doubtful case, perhaps in an early or prodromal state and perhaps not. A disease or syndrome may be manifested as a smooth continuum, as in the case of hypothyroidism or anemia, or in a more nearly binary form, "you have it or you don't," for example: rubella or pyelitis.

Diseases often, but not always, involve organ or tissue pathology visible on post mortem examination. Examples of diseases that do not involve tissue damage are migraine and idiopathic epilepsy.

The "medical model" is not different from the "psychiatric model" or the "biopsychosocial model," since the latter terms reflect aspects of medicine.

The "medical model" is an approach designed to produce change.

It is a way to conceptualize, organize and deliver assistance to an individual suffering from an illness, to families affected by a sick member, and to communities grappling with the destructive effects of a disease. It offers a conceptual approach to prevention, from which strategies may be postulated and tested. It offers a framework with which institutions and government can develop appropriate private and public policies. Finally, through public education, the medical model shapes public opinion and public expectations.

The "medical model" allows application of the institutions, systems, settings, tools and personnel devoted to medical care, medical research and public health, to the problem in question. On an individual and family level, the model means applying the customary procedures: assessment (history, examination, special tests); diagnosis; treatment planning (short- and long-term goals, therapeutic methods); ongoing evaluation and modification of the treatment plan; prognosis; and long term follow-up.

The process of diagnosis requires comparison of the patient's assessed signs and symptoms to those of a clinically recognized syndrome. In the case of compulsive gambling, the criteria for pathological gambling of the American Psychiatric Association, DSM-III, (1980), are the current standard but they will be replaced by revised criteria DSM III-R, in 1987 (APA 1986). Critics of the disease concept (for example Vatz and Weinberg, 1986) fail to understand the diagnostic process, contending that only gamblers who lose are labelled sick. They state, "If a gambler is a winner, he or she is not a 'pathological gambler' but a 'rich entrepreneur'." In fact pathological gambling *can* be diagnosed in a gambler who is winning. Signs and symptoms are present long before the overwhelming losses occur. For example, a salesman may be unable to control his impulses to gamble, spend so much of his time and interest on studying racing data that his job and marriage are failing, and be unable to account for much of his track winnings (because he gambles it on other sports). He will qualify for DSM III diagnosis even if he is still ahead financially. He will qualify under DSM III-R also (see Figure I), because of: his frequent preoccupation with gambling; his need to increase the size and frequency of his bets (whether he wins or loses); gambling when expected to fulfill job obligations; giving up important social and occupational activities in order to gamble (not servicing his customers); and continuing to gamble despite significant job and marital problems that he knows are made worse by his gambling. The fact that most pathological gamblers do not reach professional attention or accept help until they are losing does not mean that the loss defines the disease.

III THE ADDICTIVE DISEASE MODEL

Because compulsive gambling has so much in common with alcoholism and other drug addictions (e.g. Orford, 1985; Jacobs, 1986; Custer and Milt, 1985) and because these symptoms so often occur in the same people and families (Lesieur, Blume and Zoppa, 1986), compulsive or pathological gambling has been conceptualized as an addictive disease. Compulsive gamblers are often treated in programs modelled on those for addicts or in the same programs with alcohol and drug abusers (Custer, 1986, Blume 1986 a, b).

DSM-III currently groups pathological gambling under the category "Disorders of Impulse Control not Otherwise Classified," and lists criteria for diagnosis that are unlike those for alcohol or drug dependence. In the revision of the manual (DSM III-R), the diagnostic criteria for both alcohol and drug dependence on one hand, the pathological gambling on the other, have been changed. In the proposed revision the criteria are remarkably similar.

This change reflects the growing acceptance of an addiction model, which conceptualizes pathological gambling as a dependence on the "action" of gambling, in many ways similar to dependence on a mood-changing drug. The criteria reflect these similarities, including; preoccupation with the behavior, increasing "doses" (amounts and frequency of betting), the need for increased betting to achieve the desired psychological effect (tolerance), discomfort if unable to gamble (withdrawal) unsuccessful efforts to cut down or stop (loss of control), and gambling despite conflicting social expectations, important activities or negative consequences. The criteria also reflect differences, for example: chasing losses in pathological gambling; using a psychoactive substance to relieve or prevent withdrawal in substance dependence.

The addictive disease conception of compulsive gambling differs from the psychoanalytic conception, such as that advanced by Bergler

FIGURE 1
Comparison of Proposed DSM III-R Diagnostic Criteria for Substance Dependence and Pathological Gambling

Psychoactive Substance Dependence	Pathological Gambling
At least three of the following:	Maladaptive gambling behavior, as indicated by at least four of the following:
(1) when not actually using the substance, a lot of time spent looking forward to use of or arranging to get the substance	(1) frequent preoccupation with gambling or with obtaining money to gamble
(2) substance often taken in larger amounts or over a longer period than the individual intended	(2) often gambling larger amounts of money or over a longer period than intended
(3) tolerance: need for increased amounts of the substance in order to achieve intoxication or desired effect, or diminished effect with continued use of the same amount	(3) need to increase the size or frequency of bets to achieve the desired excitement
(4) characteristic withdrawal symptoms (see specific withdrawal symptoms in Psychoactive Substance-induced Organic Mental Disorders)	(4) restlessness or irritability if unable to gamble
	(5) repeated loss of money gambling and returning another day to win back losses ("chasing")
(5) substance often taken to relieve or avoid withdrawal symptoms	(6) repeated efforts to cut down or stop gambling
(6) persistent desire or repeated efforts to cut down or control substance use	(7) often gambling when expected to fulfill social or occupational obligations
(7) frequent intoxication or impairment by substance use when expected to fulfill social or occupational obligations, or when substance use is hazardous (e.g., doesn't go to work because hungover or high, goes to work high, drives when drunk)	(8) some important social, occupational, or recreational activity given up or despite other significant social, occupational, or legal problems that the individual knows to be exacerbated by gambling
(8) important social, occupational or recreational activity given up or reduced because it was incompatible with the use of the substance	(9) continuation of gambling despite inability to pay mounting debts, or despite other significant social, occupational, or legal problems that the individual knows to be exacerbated by gambling
(9) continued substance use despite a persistent social, occupational, psychological, or a physical problem that is caused or exacerbated by the use of the substance	

from: American Psychiatric Association: DSM III-R, second draft, 1986

(1957). However, both fit within the medical model. The medical model is quite flexible by nature, since it dictates no specific etiological formulation. Does this mean that any behavior of which a human being is capable can be called a disease? Is opera singing or basketball or gardening a disease? In order for a behavior pattern to fit a disease model it must be reliably and repeatedly harmful to the individual and/or others. The pattern must be characteristic for the individual and outside of full conscious control. (This differentiates kleptomania from stealing and alcoholism from drinking). It must not be a symptom of some other disease, nor an unconscious habit which can be changed by merely paying attention to the behavior. Finally, the behavior and accompanying internal state must follow a predictable course which is common to other individuals, yielding describable signs, symptoms, stages of development, and patterns of harm. Thus a single isolated episode of driving while intoxicated may cause death to the driver, but the person could not be diagnosed an alcoholic unless drinking patterns over time matched those of others with that diagnosis.

IV ADVANTAGES OF THE MEDICAL MODEL

The disease concept of pathological gambling like the disease concept of alcoholism (Blume, 1983) provides a personally and socially useful approach.

This way of thinking searches for common signs and symptoms of disease in individuals (rather than focusing on the uniqueness of each person) and uses these common features to establish a diagnosis. The diagnosis, then, allows one to predict a probable course and prognosis, and to decide which treatment would most likely benefit the patient. It is only after establishing the diagnosis that the specific gender, ethnic characteristics and circumstances of the individual become important, in formulating the treatment plan.

The disease concept is useful in lifting a large burden of irrational guilt from both patient and family. Involuntariness is part of the general idea of disease; it "happens to" one. The patient may realistically feel guilty about things he/she did or failed to do, but not about being a pathological gambler. Family members may regret certain actions, words and attitudes, but will understand that they did not cause the gambling problem.

The medical model encourages the development and financial support of resources to help pathological gamblers and their families, and to educate health care providers in identification, intervention, treatment and referral. The model encourages research on epidemiology, etiology, phenomenology, treatment and prevention. It also provides a framework for enlightened public policy in the regulation of the gambling industry, and for rational approaches to social and legal problems related to the disease. Gamblers Anonymous, a fellowship founded in 1957 on the same principles as Alcoholics Anonymous, has found the disease concept of compulsive gambling a helpful factor in recovery (Gamblers Anonymous, 1984).

Of course, there are other ways to think about the behavior of people who fit the current diagnostic criteria for pathological gambling. They may be thought of as merely unwise or uncaring. Their behavior may be seen as a special category of learned (or overlearned) behavior rather than a disease. However, neither of these conceptualizations, in my opinion, has the same social utility as the disease concept and medical model.

V OBJECTIONS TO THE MEDICAL MODEL

Some writers object to conceptualizing any psychiatric or behavioral disorder as a disease. Szasz (1974), for example, writes: "Disease or illness can affect only the body. Hence, there is no such thing as mental illness," and "Medical diagnoses are the names of genuine diseases, psychiatric diagnoses are stigmatizing labels." Szasz considers mental illness an invention of psychiatry. In his book, *Ceremonial Chemistry* (Szasz, 1985), he further develops this argument in relationship to addictive diseases. Szasz's earlier position has been effectively refuted by Guze (1977), who states,

> There is no generally accepted definition of disease adequate for all non-psychiatric disorders that would not apply equally well to psychiatric conditions. Any attempt to define disease so as to exclude most psychiatric disorders also excludes many conditions about which there is no debate as to their medical significance.

Disease concepts of psychiatric disorders have been described in varied cultures, including the Eskimo and Yoruba cultures (Murphy, 1976). In these societies psychoses and various neurotic symptoms are treated by the same healers who treat the physically ill. These syndromes are seen as something that "happens to" a person and are not the same as witchcraft or the voluntary trance of a shaman.

An additional theoretical objection is raised by Vatz and Weinberg (1986). Since loss of control (or impaired control) of behavior is central to the disease concept of compulsive gambling, they take issue with the ability of medical personnel to establish that an individual is unable to control any given behavior. Citing a psychiatric position paper on the insanity defense which states that science cannot measure "volition" or "free will," they maintain that the only evidence possible for the presence or absence of control is the "presence or absence of the behavior or the claims of the individuals who engage in these behaviors." This seems to me an argument about the basic diagnostic process in mental health: can (should) we believe what patients tell us? Hallucinations are a critical symptom in psychiatric diagnosis, yet only the individual who hears the voices knows that he/she does, and we only know because the person tells us so. Likewise, such key indicators as delusions, mood states, obsessive thoughts, and suicidal intent are based almost entirely on patients' statements. Certainly in some circumstances there may be a motivation to fake mental illness or mental health, making assessment difficult. This is especially true in criminal cases. However, the descriptions of internal experiences which become the elements of a clinical syndrome are not established from such cases. They are gleaned from the observations of clinicians and researchers working with troubled individuals who have nothing to gain by lying about their inner experiences, and have agreed to share these experiences with a hope of relief from pain. In clinical situations the professional makes a judgment about whether or not to believe that the patient is accurately communicating an internal state, and then acts accordingly. The patient's introspection, as communicated to others, is as important as behavior or bodily changes in psychiatric diagnosis.

Most other objections, seem to me to be moral in nature. The medical model is seen as a plot to absolve destructive people (in this case, compulsive gamblers) from taking responsibility for their acts. For example, Vatz and Weinberg, (1986) write, "What are the consequences of the public's acceptance of 'pathological' gambling as uncontrollable and an illness? The gambler's avoidance of responsibility for his or her actions on the one hand and status and financial support for the 'doctor' of his ailment on the other."

Others confuse the disease concept with the legal conceptualization of insanity. The two are not synonymous. Alcoholism, for example, is not a legal defense for driving while intoxicated. The importance in diagnosing a disease that bears a direct relationship to a particular crime, as alcoholism does to some cases of driving while intoxicated, and compulsive gambling does to some cases of theft or embezzlement, is that some form of treatment for the disease should be part of the sentence, if there is to be a reasonable chance for rehabilitation. Sometimes this treatment may be built into a probation or presentence diversion program. This is *not* the same as finding the individual not guilty by reason of insanity. In fact, the untreated compulsive gambler like the untreated alcoholic or addict, is particularly likely to repeat his crime, given the opportunity. Thus criminal justice policies influenced by a medical model are more likely to result in rehabilitation than those that are not.

Still others object to relieving the feelings of guilt on the part of patient and family, alluded to above. Concepts of sin and the need for confession and religious conversion would, in this model, replace illness and treatment.

In fact, although the medical model does not hold the sick person responsible for contracting the illness, it does hold him/her responsible for doing all possible to recover (see Parsons', (1951) discussion of the "sick role"). Compulsive gamblers undergoing professional treatment or in Gamblers Anonymous are encouraged to repay their debts rather than to declare bankruptcy. Making restitution to others harmed by the disease, where possible, is an integral part of the Gamblers Anonymous program.

Finally, some objections to the medical model are political. There is objection to giving the medical establishment a lead role in developing a societal response to gambling-related problems, or at least to this particular one. My only response to this position is that whatever works best in relieving suffering and improving the public wellbeing in contemporary society has a strong argument going for it. The disease concept and medical model, when applied to compulsive gambling, fits our observations and clinical experience, and offers promise for treatment, prevention and enlightened public policy. Therefore, I strongly believe we should stick with it until something that fits a lot better and offers a lot more comes along.

REFERENCES

American Psychiatric Association (1980). *Diagnostic and statistical manual of mental disorders*, 3rd edition, Washington DC, APA.
American Psychiatric Association Group to Revise DSM-III (1986). DSM-III-R in development, second draft Washington DC, APA.
Bergler, E. (1957). *The psychology of gambling*, London, International Universities Press.
Blume, S.B. (1986a). Treatment for compulsive gambling. In Levy, S.J., Blume, S.B. (Eds.) *Addictions in the Jewish community*. Federation of Jewish Philanthropies: New York.
Blume, S.B. (1986b). Treatment for the addictions: Alcoholism, drug dependence and compulsive gambling in a psychiatric setting. *Journal of Substance Abuse Treatment, 3,* 131-133.
Blume, S.B. (1983). The disease concept of alcoholism, 1983. *Journal of Psychiatric Treatment Eval, 5,* 471-478. (Also available as: Blume, S.B. (1983). *The disease concept of alcoholism today.* Johnson Institute: Minneapolis.)
Conrad P. and Schneider, J.W. (1980). *Deviance and medicalization: From badness to sickness.* CV Mosby: St. Louis.
Custer, R.L. (1986). An overview of compulsive gambling. In S.J. Levy and S.B. Blume (eds), *Addictions in the Jewish community*. Federation of Jewish Philanthropies: New York.
Custer, R.L. and Milt, H. (1985). *When luck runs out.* Facts on File: New York.
Gamblers Anonymous (1984). *Sharing recovery through Gamblers Anonymous.* Los Angeles, CA: Gamblers Anonymous Publishing.
Guze, S. (1977). The future of psychiatry: Medicine or social science? *Journal of Nervous and Mental Disorders, 165,* 225-230.
Jacobs, D.F. (1986). A general theory of addictions: A new theoretical model. *Journal of Gambling Behavior, 2,* 15-31.
Lesieur, H.R., Blume, S.B., Zoppa, R.M. (1986). Alcoholism, drug abuse and gambling. *Alcoholism Clinical and Experimental Research, 10,* 33-38.
Murphy, J.M. (1976). Psychiatric labeling in cross-cultural perspective, *Science, 191,* 139-144.
Orford, J. (1985). *Excessive Appetites:* A psychological view of addictions. Chichester: John Wiley and Sons.
Parson, T. (1951). *The Social System,* Toronto: Ontario, Collier-Macmillan, Canada.
Szasz, T. (1985). *Ceremonial chemistry: The ritual persecution of drugs, addicts and pushers.* Holmes Beach, FL: Learning Publication.
Szasz, T. (1974). *The myth of mental illness.* NY, Harper and Row.
Vatz, R.E., Weinberg, L.S. (1986). Gambling a disease? Let's call that bluff, second opinion. *Washington Post,* April 2, 1986.
World Publishing, *Webster's new international dictionary.* Unabridged, Second Edition (1966). Cleveland, OH.

The Future of Gambling Research—Learning from the Lessons of Alcoholism

Mark Dickerson
Department of Psychology, Australian National University

Some common elements in the development of the illness models of alcoholism and pathological gambling are traced. It is argued that despite strong historical parallels the gambling research literature has avoided the destructive polemics that have surrounded the erosion of the medical model of alcoholism. None-the-less it is concluded that future research into gambling will benefit from following the recent alcohol research developments particularly with regard to studying excessive gambling, not in isolated clinical populations, but in the cultural, social and legal context of all who gamble.

The result of the erosion of the medical model of alcoholism is no more clearly illustrated than in the recent UK report of the Royal College of Psychiatrists (1986) which provides a ten-point guide to *sensible drinking*. The failure of the disease theory to account for contemporary empirical data, particularly the overwhelming evidence that alcoholics may return to controlled levels of drinking (e.g. Armor, Polich & Stambul, 1976, 1978) has led to the conclusion, "that the phenomenon known as alcoholism does not betoken an *irreversible disease* but a *reversible behaviour*

Acknowledgement: to those doing research into alcohol, especially Ray Hodgson, Jim Orford and Howard Rankin who have encouraged me to learn from 'their' mistakes.

Send reprint requests to: Mark Dickerson, Ph.D., Psychology Department, Australian National University, P.O. Box 4, Canberra, A.C.T., Australia 2601.

disorder" (Heather & Robertson, 1983, p. 247). The implications of this paradigm shift range over the whole research, treatment, education, political and legal domains as they relate to drinking alcohol. It is the objective of the following discussion to highlight the historical parallels between the development of gambling and alcohol research and to present the case that the medical model of pathological gambling will become obscure not by rejection but rather by neglect.

In the context of such an argument the risk exists that the conclusion may be drawn that pathological or compulsive gamblers do not exist, that the problems of gamblers who seek help are of no consequence. Let it be noted that the work of pioneers in the field such as Bolen and Boyd (1968), Moran (1975) and Custer (1982) have demonstrated beyond dispute that excessive gambling can be associated with complex personal and social problems that may require professional help. Although the prevalence of such persons is not known, most clinicians who have had experience of helping gamblers would, regardless of their theoretical persuasion, accept the view that excessive gambling is quite appropriately categorized along with other addictive behaviors such as excessive alcohol intake, smoking, eating disorders and substance abuse (Marlatt, 1979; Miller, 1980; Orford, 1984).

The origins of the medical models of pathological gambling and alcoholism are almost identical. The dominant theme is the close association between medical practitioners and GA or AA. Jellinek's (1946, 1952) original disease conceptualization of alcoholism was based on data from a questionnaire constructed by AA and circulated to the membership via the official publication *Grapevine* (Heather & Robertson, 1983). Similarly in the UK, Moran (1975) based his typology of pathological gamblers on patients referred to a psychiatric facility, and in the US, Custer was responsible for drafting the DSM III (American Psychiatric Association, 1980) criteria for pathological gambling following in-depth studies of GA members (Custer & Custer, 1978). The schema defining the stages of the 'descent' into, and recovery from, pathological gambling and alcoholism (Custer, 1982; Jellinek, 1952, respectively) are very alike. Both models evolved from two central premises concerning loss of control and an assumed discontinuity of levels of excess between those who were sick and those who were not. An examination of how these premises became untenable for alcoholism may well provide useful lessons for the development of research into all aspects of gambling.

The demise of the medical model of alcoholism

The first assumption that the universe of drinkers could be separated into 'social' and 'pathological' was always supported more by belief than empirical data. Certainly there is now good evidence that the frequency distribution of individual alcohol consumption is continuous, positively skewed but unimodal (Heather & Robertson, 1983). The second, and by far the most important premise of the medical model of alcoholism concerned loss of control and the implicit assumption, since the treatment goal was invariably abstinence, that this loss was irreversible (Jellinek, 1952). So firmly imbedded was this assumption that the fortuitous finding that some treated alcoholics had returned to controlled levels of drinking (Davies, 1962) resulted in what can only be described as a protracted political battle. In 1969 the US National Institute of Mental Health put forward the view that no alcoholic could ever learn to drink moderately and that statements to the contrary were *unwise and dangerous* (Marlatt, 1979). Small wonder that the authors of one of the most widely known controlled drinking treatment studies, Mark and Linda Sobell (Sobell & Sobell, 1973, 1976, 1978), were accused of having falsified their data (Pendery, Maltzman & West, 1982) and despite their exoneration by a committee of enquiry (Dickens, Doob, Warwick & Winegard, 1982) TV and newspaper coverage continued, mainly to the detriment of the Sobells' reputation. This occurred despite the accumulation of a vast array of data (e.g. Armor, Polich & Stambul, 1976, 1978) supporting and clarifying the original finding by Davies (1962). If that was the dark side of the paradigm shift in alcohol research then the positive impact has been wide-ranging and significant and has been comprehensively and ably reviewed by Heather and Robertson (1983). As these authors point out the conceptualization of excessive drinking as a reversible behavior disorder has been associated with a rich literature covering a range of topics such as the determinants of loss of control and craving, empirical data on drinking behaviors in nonclinical populations and life events that influence levels of alcohol consumption. In particular, treatment research has burgeoned with the development of a whole array of methods designed to help people achieve controlled levels of drinking. Furthermore the shift from "treatment" to "learning" has usefully blurred the boundaries between clinic-based programs and educational approaches. This has resulted in a diversity of self-help materials and minimal intervention procedures. Perhaps most important of all has been the move toward an acceptance that levels of excessive drinking and their related physical and social problems (such as chronic liver disease and drunk-driving offences) are a function of the availability and general consumption of alcohol in a community and hence the result of complex of cultural, political and economic processes (Kendell, 1979; Peele, 1984).

Implications for the medical model of gambling

It will be argued below that a similar, but different sequence is occurring with respect to research into gambling. The first similarity is that there is limited but clear evidence that the universe of gamblers is not dichotomous and loss of control is not a feature that distinguishes clinical populations from high frequency gamblers in the general population. Whether the variable of interest is behavior, subjective reports or personality measures, "pathological" gamblers are similar to regular nonclinical populations of gamblers (Dickerson, 1984, 1985; Walker, 1985; Malkin, 1981, cited in Dickerson, 1984). If pathological gamblers do not form a relatively distinct group this fact alone contradicts one of the three fundamental assumptions of DSM III (Spitzer & Williams, 1980) and challenges the inclusion of pathological gambling within such a classificatory system. Such theoretical niceties may be substantiated by what is actually taking place.

Contemporary surveys of research published in the first volume of the *Journal of Gambling Behavior* and in the proceedings of recent conferences in the US and Australia (Eadington, 1985; Caldwell, *et. al.*, 1985; McMillen, 1985a) suggest that ongoing gambling research and theory goes well beyond the bounds of a medical model. Although there is not as strong and rich a literature as presently exists for alcohol, some studies have signposted important future directions for research. Igor Kusyszyn has been in the forefront of researchers advocating and completing studies with populations of normal gamblers (Kusyszyn & Rubenstein, 1985). A seminal study by Anderson & Brown (1984) confirmed the relevance of focussing on such gamblers by highlighting the potential role of physiological arousal in persistent gambling. Their results also confirmed that findings from laboratory gambling games were likely to have little relevance to the understanding of the psychological processes involved in real world gambling environments.

Even in those areas where the medical model might have been expected to exert greatest influence, namely loss of control and processes determining excess, there exist a limited but diverse range of explanatory models (e.g. Abt, McGurrin & Smith, 1985; Brown, 1986; Dickerson & Adcock, 1986; McConaghy, 1980). There is a dearth of comparative treatment outcome studies (Blaszczynski, 1985) and the first exploration of a minimal intervention approach is currently in progress (Dickerson & Hinchy, 1986a). Educational and public awareness programs paralleling the recent advice in the UK regarding sensible drinking (Royal College of Psychiatrists, 1986) do not exist although one attempt has been made to popularize in book form a controlled approach to all forms of gambling (Allcock & Dickerson, 1986). Socio-political studies of the decision processes governing the introduction of new forms of legalized gambling has seen limited attention (McMillen, 1985b) and prevalence studies of excessive gambling are virtually unknown (Dickerson & Hinchy, 1986b). Despite very obvious gaps in current research the point to be emphasized here is that the existence of a medical model of gambling has *not* led to a widely held set of beliefs that have restricted research.

Have then the destructive polemics of the alcoholism debate been avoided? If the answer is yes, then some of the contributing factors may be the slow development of gambling research (Bolen, 1974), resistance by the medical profession itself to the illness conception of gambling (Editorial, British Medical Journal, 1968) and the absence of a psychoactive agent. Furthermore, compared with the illness model of alcoholism, the role of loss of control was not so firmly established as the keystone of the model. The original DSM III (American Psychiatric Association, 1980) criteria A specified fairly loosely that "the individual is chronically and progressively unable to resist impulses to gamble." In the proposed revisions (Blume, 1987; Lesieur, in press) this has been replaced by several alternative items that relate more specifically to control of gambling expenditure, chasing losses and repeated attempts to stop or cut back. Neither set of definitions necessarily imply that the loss of control is irreversible and that therefore the treatment goal must be abstinence. This was the focus of controversy in alcoholism. In contrast, research into the treatment of excessive gambling has either implicitly (Peck & Ashcroft, 1972, cited in Dickerson, 1984) or explicitly addressed the treatment goal of controlled gambling (Dickerson & Weeks, 1979) and some contemporary hospital based programs in both the US and Australia do not insist on abstinence (Blaszczynski, 1985).

It could be argued that the medical model of gambling has been sustained by two factors. The first, but not necessarily the most influential, has been the close links between GA and those hospital-based programs providing treatment for excessive gamblers. Certainly GA would appear to be the immediate "losers" should there be some decree that excessive gambling is not an illness. However it is more likely that some gamblers will continue to prefer to consider their problem in illness terms and, as for alcohol, there will be those for whom the goal of abstinence is preferred and appropriate (Heather and Robertson, 1983). In the meantime hospital-based programs of treatment remain the dominant source of research reports on excessive gambling thereby sustaining the notion of "pathology." The second factor that indirectly maintains this illness approach is the very slow development of research programs with a community data base that can challenge the assumptions of the medical model. Within psychology this can be attributed to the slow acceptance that laboratory games provided few insights into real life gambling (Anderson & Brown, 1984), and also to the emphasis on publication rate that makes field research a less preferred option (Phares, 1984).

The research program at the Australian National University now entering its 5th year not only illustrates the feasibility of conducting such community-oriented field work research but also the real scope for advancing our state of knowledge. In an urban community totalling 200,000 people with many legalized forms of gambling, three complimentary strands of research have been developed each of which is to some extent sustained by the goodwill and acceptance of people who gamble and those who own and manage the gambling industry.

There is no casino, but there is easy access to continuous forms of gambling such as poker machines and off-course betting. Both have been shown to be linked with excessive gambling (Cornish, 1978; Dickerson, 1984; Orford, 1984). The research includes descriptive surveys by interview and questionnaire (Dickerson, Fabre & Bayliss, 1985), personality correlates of loss of control such as chasing (Dickerson, Hinchy & Fabre, 1986), estimates of the prevalence of excessive gambling (Dickerson & Hinchy, 1986b), empirical studies of individual sessions of poker machine play (Dickerson & Adcock, 1986; Leary & Dickerson, 1985), and a controlled evaluation of a free minimal intervention program of help for excessive gamblers (Dickerson & Hinchy, 1986a). The empirical studies of volunteer gamblers has developed a methodology that permits the unobtrusive, simultaneous collection of physiological, subjective and behavioral/event data streams for periods of up to two and a half hours (Dickerson, Hinchy, Schaefer, Whitworth & Fabre, 1986). Even the informal or anecdotal data from such a program is rich and conflicts with simplistic illness conceptions. For example, some of our volunteers, whose weekly rate of financial losses were very similar to excessive gamblers seeking help, have been observed to reduce or give up without any intervention. (Similar findings for alcoholism were established by Saunders and Kershaw (1979).) Some have continued at a frequent, costly, but controlled level, and two prospective volunteers, having described their gambling behavior, chose instead to enter the minimal intervention program. All our experience contradicts the supposed dichotomy of social and pathological gamblers. In such a research environment to adopt the medical model of gambling would be akin to self-imposed myopia. It is this perspective that leads to the conclusion that the medical model requires no formal rejection. It will simply fall into desuetude.

In conclusion, parallels have been drawn between the origins of the medical models of alcoholism and gambling and their respective impact on subsequent research developments. Despite historical similarities it was argued that the medical model of gambling has exerted only a weak restrictive effect even on treatment research and that its demise will not therefore be followed by the destructive debate that has occurred in relation to alcoholism. It was proposed that the literature on gambling already showed some limited but healthy signs of examining all aspects of gambling from economic to political. The most important lesson to be learned from the alcoholism debate must surely be the importance of examining the nature of excessive gambling, its parameters and underlying processes, *in the context of all who gamble.*

REFERENCES

Abt, V., McGurrin, M.C. & Smith, J.F. (1985). Toward a synoptic model of gambling behavior. *Journal of Gambling Behavior, 1,* 2, 79–88.
Allcock, C. & Dickerson, M. (1986). *The Guide to Good Gambling.* Social Science Press: Wentworth Falls, Australia.
American Psychiatric Association (1980). *Diagnostic and Statistical Manual of Mental Disorders* (3rd

ed.) DSM-III. American Psychiatric Association: Washington, DC.
Anderson, G. & Brown, R.I.F. (1984). Real and laboratory gambling, sensation-seeking and arousal. *British Journal of Psychology, 75,* 401–410.
Armor, D.J., Polich, J.M. & Stambul, H.B. (1976). *Alcoholism and Treatment.* Rand Corporation: Santa Monica.
Armor, D.J., Polich, J.M. & Stambul, H.B. (1978). *Alcoholism and Treatment.* Rand Corporation: Santa Monica.
Blaszczynski, A. (1985). Treatment approaches for the control of pathological gambling. In Caldwell G., Dickerson, M.G., Haig, B. & Sylvan L. (eds.) *Gambling in Australia.* Croom Helm: Sydney.
Blume, S.B. (1987). Compulsive gambling and the medical model. *Journal of Gambling Behavior, 3,* (this issue).
Bolen, D.W. (1974). Gambling: historical highlights, trends and their implications for contemporary society. Paper presented at the First Annual Conference on Gambling, Las Vegas.
Bolen, D.W. & Boyd, W.H. (1968). Gambling and the gambler. *Archives of General Psychiatry, 18,* 617–30.
Brown, R.I.F. (1986). Gambling addictions, arousal and affective decision making explanations of behavioural reversions or relapses. *International Journal of Addiction* (in press).
Caldwell, G., Dickerson, M.G., Haig, B. & Sylvan, L. (eds.) (1985). *Gambling in Australia.* Croom Helm: Sydney.
Cornish, D.B. (1978). *Gambling: a review of the literature and its implications for policy and research.* HMSO: London.
Custer, R.L. (1982). An overview of compulsive gambling. In Carone, P.A., Yolles, S.F., Kieffer, S.N. & Krinsky, L.W. (Eds.) *Addictive Disorders Update.* Human Sciences Press, New York.
Custer, R.L. & Custer, L.F. (1978). Characteristics of the recovering compulsive gambler: a survey of 150 members of Gamblers Anonymous. Paper presented at the Fourth Annual Conference on Gambling, Nevada.
Davies, D.L. (1962). Normal drinking in recovered alcohol addicts. *Quarterly Journal of Studies on Alcohol, 24,* 321–332.
Dickens, B.M., Doob, A.N., Warwick, O.H. & Winegard, W.C. (1982). Report of the Committee of Enquiry into Allegations Concerning Drs. Linda and Mark Sobell. Information Centre, Addiction Research Foundation, 33 Russell Street, Toronto, M5S, 2S1, Ontario, Canada.
Dickerson, M.G. (1984). *Compulsive Gamblers,* Longman: London.

Dickerson, M.G. (1985). The characteristics of the compulsive gambler: a rejection of a typology. In G. Caldwell, M.G. Dickerson, B. Haig, & L. Sylvan, (eds.) *Gambling in Australia.* Croom Helm: Sydney.
Dickerson, M.G. & Adcock, S.G. (1986). Mood, arousal and cognitions in persistent gambling: preliminary investigation of a theoretical model. *Journal of Gambling Behavior, 1,* 3–15.
Dickerson, M.G., Fabre, J. & Bayliss, D. (1985). A comparison of TAB customers and poker machine players. In J. McMillen (ed.) *Gambling in the 80's.* Griffith University Reprographics:Brisbane.
Dickerson, M.G. & Hinchy, J. (1986a). Minimal treatment intervention for problem gamblers. In M. Walker (ed.) *Faces of Gambling.* Harper and Row: Sydney.
Dickerson, M.G. & Hinchy, J. (1986b). The prevalence of excessive and pathological gambling in Australia. Submitted to *Journal of Gambling Behavior.*
Dickerson, M.G., Hinchy, J. & Fabre, J. (1986). Chasing, arousal and sensation seeking in off-course gambling. *British Journal of Addiction* (in press).
Dickerson, M.G., Hinchy, J., Schaefer, M., Whitworth, N. & Fabre, J. (1986). The use of a hand-held micro-computer in the collection of physiological subjective and behavioural data in ecologically valid settings. Submitted to Behaviour Research and Therapy.
Dickerson, M.G. & Weeks, D. (1979). Controlled gambling as a therapeutic technique for compulsive gamblers. *Journal of Behavior Therapy and Experimental Psychiatry, 10,* 139–41.
Eadington, W.R. (Ed.) (1985). *The Gambling Studies:* proceedings of the Sixth National Conference on Gambling and Risk Taking. Bureau of Business and Economic Research, College

of Business Administration, University of Nevada, Reno.
Editors. (1968). Editorial on compulsive gambling. *British Medical Journal, 2,* 69.
Heather, N. & Robertson, I. (1983). *Controlled Drinking.* Methuen, London.
Jellinek, E.M. (1946). Phases in the drinking history of alcoholics. *Quarterly Journal of Studies on Alcohol, 7,* 1-88.
Jellinek, E.M. (1952). Phases of alcohol addiction. *Quarterly Journal of Studies on Alcohol, 13,* 673-684.
Kendell, R.E. (1979). Alcoholism: a medical or a political problem. *British Medical Journal, i,* 367-71.
Kusyszyn, I. & Rubenstein, L. (1985). Locus of control and race track betting behaviors: a preliminary investigation. *Journal of Gambling Behavior, 1,* 106-110.
Leary, K. & Dickerson, M.G. (1985). Levels of arousal in high- and low-frequency gamblers. *Behaviour Research and Therapy, 23,* 635-40.
Lesieur, H.R. (in press). Altering the DSM-III criteria for pathological gambling. *Journal of Gambling Behavior.*
Malkin, D. (1981). An empirical investigation into some aspects of problem gambling. Unpublished Masters thesis: University of Western Australia.
Marlatt, G.A. (1979). Alcohol use and problem drinking: a cognitive-behavioral analysis. In P.C. Kendall, and S.D. Hollon (eds.) *Cognitive Behavioral Interventions, Theory Research and Procedures.* Academic Press: London.
McConaghy, N. (1980). Behaviour completion mechanisms rather than primary drives maintain behavioural patterns. *Activitas Nervosa Superior* (Praha), *22,* 138-51.
McMillen, J. (Ed.) (1985a). *Gambling in the 80's.* Griffith University Reprographics: Brisbane.
McMillen, J. (1985b). Casino gambling in Queensland: prospects, problems and paradoxes. In G. Caldwell, M.G. Dickerson, B. Haig, & L. Sylvan, (eds.) *Gambling in Australia.* Croom Helm: Sydney.
Miller, W.R. (ed.) (1980). *The Addictive Behaviors: Treatment of Alcoholism, Drug Abuse, Smoking and Obesity.* Pergamon: Oxford.
Moran, E. (1975). Pathological gambling. In *British Journal of Psychiatry,* Special Publication No. 9: *Contemporary Psychiatry,* Royal College of Psychiatrists, London.
Orford, J. (1984). *Excessive appetites: a psychological view of addictions.* Wiley: New York.
Peck, D.F. & Ashcroft, J.B. (1972). The use of stimulus satiation in the modification of habitual gambling. Proceedings of the Second British and European Association Conference on Behavior Modification, Kilkenny, Ireland.
Peele, S. (1984). The cultural context of psychological approaches to alcoholism. *American Psychologist, 39,* 1337-1351.
Pendery, M.L., Maltzman, I.M. & West, L.J. (1982). Controlled drinking by alcoholics? New findings and a re-evaluation of a major affirmative study. *Science, 217,* 169-75.
Phares, E.J. (1984). *Introduction to Personality.* Merrill, Sydney.
Royal College of Psychiatrists (1986). *Alcohol our favorite drug;* report of a special committee of the Royal College of Psychiatrists. Tavistock Press: London.
Saunders, W.M. & Kershaw, P.W. (1979). Spontaneous remission from alcoholism—a community study. *British Journal of Addiction, 74,* 251-65.
Sobell, M.B. & Sobell, L.C. (1973). Individualized behavior therapy for alcoholics. *Behavior Therapy, 4,* 49-72.
Sobell, M.B. & Sobell, L.C. (1976). Second-year treatment outcome of alcoholics treated by individualized behavior therapy: results. *Behaviour Research and therapy, 14,* 195-215.
Sobell, M.B. & Sobell, L.C. (1978). *Behavioral Treatment of Alcohol Problems.* Plenum: New York.
Spitzer, R.L. & Williams, J.B.W. (1980). Classification of mental disorders and DSM III. In H.I. Kaplan, A.M. Freedman, & J.B.W. Williams (eds.) *Comprehensive Textbook of Psychiatry III.* Williams and Wilkins, Baltimore.
Walker, M.B. (1985). Explanations for Gambling. In G. Caldwell, M.G. Dickerson, B. Haig, L. Sylvan (eds.) *Gambling in Australia.* Croom Helm: Sydney.

Pathological Gambling:
A Parsimonious Need State Model

Richard A. McCormick, Ph.D.
Cleveland VA Medical Center

The model proposed attempts to integrate the growing data base on pathological gamblers in a parsimonious manner. The model focuses on psychological observations, although it recognizes the parallel importance of physiological phenomena. The model is based on two recurring observations with pathological gamblers: Gambling satisfies recurring and often intensified needs for the gambler; and pathological gamblers vary tremendously on a number of dimensions. The model suggests that attempts to understand pathological gambling must focus on sub-types of pathological gamblers. Two sub-types, are discussed.

INTRODUCTION

This paper attempts to integrate the growing data base on pathological gambling into a model which worships at the altar of no theory or guild, one that has neither political nor professional motives. It attempts only to explain what we know about pathological gambling in the simplist, most parsimonious manner. The model focuses on psychological observations, since this is the level of abstraction where we currently have the most data on gambling behavior. In describing the model I have attempted to acknowledge that there are physiological underpinnings to the psychological phenomenon discussed. When possible I have discussed promising research directions for increasing our knowledge base about the physiological factors at play in pathological gambling. I strongly believe that a psychological model is not in competition with a physiological model. The psychological and physiological explanations

---

Send reprint requests to: Richard A. McCormick, Ph.D., Psychology Service, V.A. Medical Center, 10,000 Brecksville Road, Brecksville, Ohio 44141.

for gambling ought to complement and be consistent with one another.

The development and description of the model revolve around two basic observations.

Observation I: Gambling is a behavior, a behavior which has effects on the gambler.

We can choose to conceptualize these "effects" in either psychological or physiological terms. Every psychological effect, after all, has its physiological parallel and vice versa. If these effects meet some need (which is another way of saying "adjust some imbalance," or "provide some reward," or "give relief") in the person then the behavior may be repeated. If the need is ongoing and even intensifies, then the gambling behavior may be repeated at an increasing frequency hence, the "addictive" quality of pathological gambling.

Many behaviors could be substituted in the paragraph above without changing its truth — sexual promiscuity, violence, drug and alcohol consumption to name but a few. People who practice these behaviors repeatedly, even when the effect is to cause havoc in their lives, seem to be similar to each other on measurable personality dimensions. For example, personality studies of gamblers show that, as a group, they are very similar to other addicted samples (e.g. Graham & Lowenfeld, 1986; McCormick, Taber, Kruedelbach, & Russo, in press). Furthermore, gamblers seem to share a common familial background with other addicted individuals and cross addictions are common (e.g. Ramirez, McCormick, Russo, Taber, 1983). Although in the case of substance abuse, an exogenous chemical is added with its own effects that potentiate or compound the physiological effects of the drug taking behavior, the basic process of meeting needs is the same.

An important correlary to observation I is that gambling behavior and its effects can be used by a variety of different people to satisfy a host of different needs. This leads us to a consideration of the next observation.

Observation II: Pathological gamblers vary tremendously.

The more we study pathological gamblers as a group the clearer this finding becomes; well controlled studies of personality measures underscore it (e.g. Graham & Lowenfeld, 1986; McCormick, Taber, Kruedelbach & Russo, in press). All pathological gamblers aren't gregarious, they vary. Some in fact are shy and withdrawn. All pathological gamblers aren't narcissistic, they vary. Some have an overly rigid sense of interpersonal responsibility as well as value systems which torment them with guilt. All pathological gamblers aren't intelligent, they vary. Many measure in the average range on standardized intelligence tests, some lower. The only generalization that seems to hold is that they all gamble, and that their gambling causes them significant problems.

This fact, the interpersonal variance among gamblers, is a problem for model builders. Model building, after all, is a generalization process. A model attempts to help us consolidate information. It tries to provide a theoretical framework from which reliable and valid generalizations flow. A model helps the clinician or scientist handle large volumes of data.

The highest level of generalization, "all pathological gamblers," is seductive. It seems to be the simplest and to encompass the largest number of people. It therefore has great attraction if one is trying to make a point to the public or to a political body. However, in developing an explanatory model for pathological gambling the level of generalization must be carefully scrutinized. The facts, and the knowledge we deduce from those facts, don't allow us to build a model at the highest level of generalization that is more than descriptive — at least not yet. Some lower level of generalization is more likely to provide useful insights into the causation and process of pathological gambling.

The current data base does support generalization at the level of subtypes, and there may be both explanatory value and clinical utility to conceptualizing subtypes of pathological gamblers. Subtyping could be done based on any number of dimensions. For example, it could be based on the nature of the gambling experience (casino, horse racing, stock market, etc.), or based on the frequency or duration of gambling.

The model suggested here delineates subtypes based on the need state that the effects of gambling behavior adjust. The model is consistent with observation I. It focuses on the importance of gambling behavior in meeting recurring, repetitive needs of the pathological gambler. It also is consistent with observation II. It focuses on a level of generalization below that of "all pathological gamblers."

SELECTED SUBTYPES OF PATHOLOGICAL GAMBLERS

Two from among an unknown number of subtypes of pathological gamblers are to be discussed. They were chosen because the data are clearest for them. Gamblers qualify for inclusion in one of the subtypes because they are similar to other members of the subtype in the need that gambling satisfies. Thus, the central dimension for the model's subtyping is the nature of the gambler's need state.

Subtype A: The recurringly depressed pathological gambler

As clinicians have long recognized, some pathological gamblers are depressed when entering treatment. Recent, more carefully controlled studies (e.g. McCormick, Russo, Ramirez, & Taber, 1984; Taber, McCormick, Russo, Adkins & Ramirez, In Press) verify this fact, and also demonstrate that for a significant number of these gamblers the depression is a lifelong pattern which may precede their gambling. Many of these patients have a history of significant life trauma (Taber, McCormick, & Ramirez, 1987). Our more recent work has established that patients in this subtype have a depressogenic cognitive style which is longstanding and pervasive in their lives. They attribute negative events to internal causation (i.e. they blame themselves), often to an unrealistic degree. They generalize the impact of a setback in one part of their life to other parts, and they feel that things have always been bad and will continue to be so. Very preliminary data suggest that these gamblers may display measurable differences on biochemical measures, when compared to nondepressed gamblers and euthymic normals.

The depressogenic cognitive style, paralleled perhaps by a biochemical imbalance, creates what is perceived by the gambler as a strong and enduring need state. He or she feels repeatedly or cyclically depressed and agitated. The effects of gambling behavior produce a noticeable change in this need state. The gambler describes feeling better while gambling, even euphoric. The process for this perceived change can be explained in either psychological terms or biological terms. In psychological terms, the gambler's attention is focused on the all consuming high arousal gambling activity. The high stimulus environment of the casino or track may further reinforce the escape to this alternative perceptual world. Attention is focused on the anticipation and experience of gambling. Gambling could be the perfect "get away from it all" vacation, but for the problem that it happens every day.

If we choose to focus on the biological parallel to this psychological experience, we can note that high arousal, stressful behavior causes immediate biochemical changes. Research with other populations has demonstrated that these changes include endocrine secretions, notably endorphins and cortisol (Dubois, Pickar, Cohen, MacNamara, & Bunney, 1981). Endorphin secretion could be the biological underpinning of the euphoria the gambler reports, or the altered state of consciousness that is experienced as part of the gambler's perceptual focusing on the gambling task. High arousal behavior also has been shown to increase peripherally measured catecholamines. Catecholamine deficiencies have been implicated as the biological correlate of the state of depression (Van Praag, 1982).

According to a need state model the gambler discovers that gambling behavior produces psychological/biological changes that reduce the need state. Gambling then becomes one option when struggling with the unpleasant state. This process may work well for the situationally depressed person who is rejuvenated and refreshed by his or her gambling vacation. Unfortunately, a stronger and more enduring need state, such as we find in the chronically depressed person, sets off an addictive cycle. The temporary psychological relief or readjustment of a biological imbalance is finite and followed by a rebound need state that is of greater intensity than the original need state.

The rebound need state can also be explained either in psychological or physiological terms. The problems that the gambler sought to forget are still there when he or she finishes gambling, in fact they are often magnified because more money has been lost or more responsibilities neglected. The gambler processes this real deterioration in his/her condition through a depressogenic cognitive style and the perceived catastrophy is magnified further. Physiologically, the organism has a strong tendency to maintain homeostasis. When catecholamine secretion is repeatedly increased through the high arousal behavior, changes occur at the receptor sites for these catecholamines which can result in further depletion, below the pregambling level, when the gambling stops. For the endocrine secretions a tolerance effect may occur where greater stimulation is required to cause the same endocrine response. The net effect of this psychological and/or physiological rebound is that the gambler feels worse, the need state is increased.

And so the cycle continues. As the need state increases the gambler may see fewer options for relieving it. This may be due to reality factors (e.g. running out of sources to earn money, or friends feeling used and exiting) or due to an increasing fixation on the most potent and recent means for satisfying need. Here we have the cycle of decreasing options elucidated by Lesieur (1979).

Subtype B: The chronically understimulated gambler.

A subset of gamblers, while they may feel temporarily down, experience very little strong affect. What these gamblers do verbalize is a sense of frequent boredom — a strong, enduring need for almost constant excitement and stimulation. These gamblers are markedly different than the depressogenic gambler in many regards. They seem not to have a strong internalized value system, they are generally gregarious, and they may be quite narcissistic. Their impulse control is poor, even when compared with other pathological gamblers. Their lack of control is generally pervasive in their lives. Unlike the depressed gambler who may have periods of vocational stability, for example, the high stimulation-seeking gambler has generally been able to exert little control in any aspect of his or her life. Hyperactivity, low frustration tolerance and a constant search for novel arousal are their hallmark characteristics.

Gambling satiates the need state for these pathological gamblers, but only for a short time. The rebound phenomenon in this subtype is more a function of the tolerance effect than is the case with the depressed gambler. The "action" becomes boring unless it is novel and increasingly arousing. Furthermore, gambling is inherently a highly arousing activity. In reality terms it is difficult for most life experiences to match it for moment to moment intensity. Consequently, the number of options perceived as useful to relieve the boredom need-state quickly narrows as the tolerance effect sets in. Few other life activities can surpass the threshold of arousal intensity necessary to reduce the need state.

CONCLUSION

I have attempted to put forward a model for pathological gambling which is consistent with our current level of knowledge about the phenomenon. The model is deliberately simple. There are those who might say that we can create models at a higher level of generalization. The psychoanalysts might theorize, for example, that the two subtypes outlined here are merely phenotypes of the same genotype, that deep-seated feelings of inferiority and guilt energize both subtypes. The narcissistic gambler is merely highly defended against such feelings. I would caution that there is potential peril in jumping to a higher level of abstraction before the data are complete. Such a jump can cause real and significant variation to be lost in the averaging process. If some gamblers are strongly depressed and others are just as strongly defended against any perception of depression, then as a group they may not appear any more depressed, on the average, than any other group where everyone is generally in the middle.

Others may say that my level of generalization is too high, that perhaps these subtypes have more important differences than they have commonalities. Surely this is an empirical question which time will answer.

My model is simple because our level of knowledge is limited. The model is general enough to be consistent with much of our current data, yet hopefully it stretches imagination just enough to raise testable questions. The model recognizes that the continuing arguments over whether psychological or physiological forces are primary is specious. The two are in the facets of a single phenomenon. It may be temporarily expedient for us to discuss them as though they were separate "things" that could vary independently. This expedience may be necessary to foster research which eventually leads to our understanding how we, psychobiological creatures that we are, function. However, we are deceived if we forget that this separation is a mere expedient and if we accept as true the separation of the psychological from the physiological.

REFERENCES

Dubois, M., Pickar, D., Cohen, M.R., Roth, Y.F., MacNamara, T.B., & Bunney, W.E. (1981). Surgical stress is accompanied by an increase in plasma beta-endorphin immunoreactivity. *Life Sciences, 29,* 1249-1254.

Graham, J.R. & Lowenfeld, B.H. (1986). Personality dimensions of the pathological gambler. *Journal of Gambling Behavior, 2*(1), 58-66.

Lesieur, H.R. (1979). The compulsive gambler's spiral of options and involvement. *Psychiatry, 42,* 79-87.

McCormick, R.A., Russo, A.M., Ramirez, L.F., & Taber, J.I. (1984). Affective disorders among pathological gamblers seeking treatment. *American Journal of Psychiatry, 141,* 215-218.

McCormick, R.A., Taber, J.I., Kruedelbach, N.B., & Russo, A.M.: Personality profiles of pathological gamblers: The California Personality Inventory. *Journal of Clinical Psychology,* in press.

Ramirez, L.F., McCormick, R.A., Russo, A.M. & Taber, J.I. (1983). Patterns of substance abuse in pathological gamblers undergoing treatment. *Addictive Behaviors, 8,* 425-428.

Taber, J.I., McCormick, R.A., & Ramirez, L.F. (1987). The prevalence and impact of major life stressors among pathological gamblers. *The International Journal of the Addictions, 22,* 71-79.

Taber, J.I., McCormick, R.A., Russo, A., Adkins, B.J. & Ramirez, L.F., Pathological gamblers following treatment: An outcome study. *American Journal of Psychiatry,* in press.

Wray, I. & Dickerson, M.G. (1981). Cessation of high frequency gambling and "withdrawal" symptoms. *British Journal of Addiction, 76,* 401-405.

Economic Perceptions of Gambling Behavior

William R. Eadington

Professor of Economics, University of Nevada, Reno

This article outlines the structure of orthodox consumer theory in economics, and reviews the major applications to gambling behavior. Gambling as a means to achieve higher desired levels of wealth is discussed, as is gambling as a consumption activity, as an end in itself. The question of rationality and gambling is discussed, and implications for public policy toward gambling, as it relates to economic models of gambling behavior, are presented.

INTRODUCTION

Generally speaking, models of rational economic behavior by consumers have been developed for the purpose of providing a framework of analysis to generate insights into how consumers, as a group, will react to changes in economic conditions in their planned purchases of the various commodities available to them. The framework is developed around the fundamental assumptions that consumers are self-interested, goal oriented, and rational. They purchase and consume commodities for the ultimate purpose of generating "utility" or satisfaction. The consumer derives utility by allocating a monetary budget over the range

---

Send reprint requests to: William R. Eadington, Ph.D., Professor of Economics, University of Nevada, Reno, Nevada 89557.

of alternative commodity bundles in such a manner as to end up with the most preferred available bundle; at this point it is said that utility is maximized.

This methodology leads to a conceptual framework from which hypothetical demand schedules for the various available commodities can be derived. The parameters which are treated as "givens" include the tastes and preferences of the individual consumers, the magnitudes of the constraining factors (i.e. how much income consumers have to allocate), and the prices of the various commodities. The formalized problem is often stated in mathematical terms: a consumer must choose the amounts of the various commodities to be consumed in such a manner as to maximize utility, subject to the limitations imposed by a finite amount of money in the relevant planning period. (See, for example, Henderson and Quandt, 1980, chapter 2.) The solution to the optimizing problem can then be mathematically manipulated to generate a demand schedule, which predicts the amount of each commodity that will be acquired as a function of that commodity's price, the price of all other commodities, and the given level of consumer income. The demand schedule can be conceptually constructed for each consumer individually, and then the individual demand schedules can be aggregated over all consumers to determine the market demand for any particular commodity.

After reviewing the existing literature on gambling behavior, one might not expect that the calculating and rational framework of consumer behavior as developed in economic theory could offer much meaningful insight into the actual behavior of the gambler, behavior that is complex and sometimes apparently irrational. Furthermore, when the discussion stretches into the area of pathological gambling, the concept of rationality that economic models take for granted must clearly come into question. Nonetheless, both the economic model of consumer behavior and a number of applications of that model to the gambler and risk taker can offer insights and perspectives that do not easily flow from the medical, psychological, or sociological descriptions of gambling behavior. It is the intent of this article to point out some of those insights, and to demonstrate the usefulness of the application of the economic model, one that is basically a simplistic model in psychological terms, but one that relies on explicit goal-oriented rational behavior, as a contributor to the understanding of both normal and deviant gambling behavior.

ECONOMIC MODELS OF GAMBLING BEHAVIOR

In order to extend the model of rational economic behavior into the world of consumers contemplating the purchase of lotto tickets or placing wagers at the race track, a few modifications must be made. The most obvious change from the standard framework is the fact that the *ex ante* price of a wager or sequence of wagers (which is typically defined as the mathematical expected loss to the bettor of the wager or wagers) will differ from the *ex post* price (reflecting the actual average outcomes of wagers) in the short run, but the two prices, on average, will tend to converge in the long run. Indeed, it is the possibility (and the hope) that the *ex post* price will diverge significantly in the positive direction from the bettor's expected loss that creates interest in the wagers. In effect, the gambler is buying "action" by making wagers, but the actual price paid will not be known until after the wagering has been completed.

Though consumer theory does not try to look into the individual's utility function to determine deeper motivations in the formulation of tastes and preferences, it has been common to dichotomize between two basic motivations for gambling: the hope of achieving higher levels of wealth (the wealth motivation, or gambling as investment), and utility derived from the actual participation in the gambling activities (the entertainment motivation, or gambling as consumption) (Eadington, 1975; Ignatin and Smith, 1976). Most economic analysis has centered on the wealth motivation as the sole factor influencing the consumer's gambling decisions (Friedman and Savage, 1946; Brenner, 1983); however, there have been a few attempts to broaden the analysis to include the entertainment motivation (Eadington, 1973; Tsukahara and Brumm, 1976).

When the economic justification for gambling is based on the wealth motivation, three lines of argument have been made. The first of these is based on the premise that the marginal utility of wealth diminishes as an individual becomes more wealthy; an incremental contribution to wealth means more to an individual when wealth is limited than when it is abundant. In this case, gambling for the wealth motive is irrational, because even if the wagers offered were fair (i.e. had no expected loss), the expected utility of the gamble would be negative. And, according to the strict criteria of the consumer behavior model, no "economic man" would freely and willingly accept a decline in his level of utility, because there is no self-interest in doing so (Marshall, 1930, p. 843; Hardy, 1923, p. 128).

The second and most frequently cited of the arguments using the wealth motivation (Friedman and Savage, 1948) postulates that the simultaneous participation by the same individual in gambling markets (accepting a negative expectation for the right to participate in a lottery which offers a small probability of winning a large prize that would bring about a significantly higher level of wealth), and in insurance markets (accepting a negative expectation for the right to protect oneself against events that carry a small probability of significant losses) point out an asymmetry in one's utility of wealth. The individual is exhibiting a diminishing marginal utility of wealth for levels of wealth below the status quo, but increasing marginal utility of wealth for levels of wealth above the current level.

The insurance purchase is interpreted as follows. Insurance has a negative actuarial expectation to the purchaser, but because the purchase is made, its acquisition *must* increase the purchaser's expected utility. In order for the expected utility of the insured situation to exceed the expected utility of the gamble involving the possibility of a financially catastrophic event, the shape of the individual's utility of wealth curve must be concave from below, i.e. the expected utility of not being insured, involving a gamble on wealth that could be lost versus avoiding the cost of the premium, is less than the actual utility of the individual's status quo wealth less the cost of the insurance premium. In this context, such an individual is risk-averse on the downside, willing to pay, on average, to avoid the risks that insurance covers.

On the other hand, the purchase of a lottery ticket which offers a small probability at a large prize must also be accepted as a rational act, because the rational individual is making the decision in light of the obvious mathematical expected loss of the gamble. This action implies the expected utility of the lottery, involving changes to the individual's status quo wealth in the form of a gamble on the prize that could be won versus the cost of the lottery ticket, exceeds the actual utility of the gambler's status quo situation. In order for this calculus to hold together, the gambler must experience *increasing* marginal utility of wealth for levels of wealth above the current level.

When someone buys both insurance and lottery tickets, that individual is paying, on average, for the opportunity to gamble on the chance of a significantly higher level of wealth, but at the same time, is also paying to avoid a gamble that poses the possibility of a significantly lower level of wealth.

Interestingly, it was not the primary intent of Friedman and Savage to describe the behavior of gamblers, but rather to describe decision-making under conditions of risk. One of their objectives was to undermine the theoretical support for the concept of diminishing marginal utility of wealth, which had long been used as a justification for progressive income taxes and confiscatory inheritance taxes.

A third type of analysis that utilizes the wealth motivation argues that an individual's utility depends not only on the absolute level of wealth, but also on one's wealth relative to other members of society (Tec, 1964; Brenner, 1983; Brenner, 1985). This approach implies that gambling can be an efficient means of upward economic mobility for some members of society because there may be no other options available to them with which to achieve certain higher levels of wealth. However, protecting one's wealth via insurance may also be the most efficient means of preserving a desired economic state, and the individual may be willing to pay the price to avoid significant wealth reductions.

This framework does away with some of the more strained results of the Friedman/Savage approach, and does not mandate conclusions concerning increasing or decreasing marginal utilities of wealth. Rather, the model implies that a person's propensity to participate in lottery-type gambles will be greater the lower the absolute level of wealth, and the lower the relative level of wealth; a person's propensity to insure against significant reductions in wealth will be greater the higher the absolute level of wealth, and the higher the relative level of wealth.

There are a number of testable hypotheses that follow from the implications of this model. Brenner predicts that "the relatively poor will plan to spend a greater fraction of their wealth on lotteries than the relatively rich, and that people of all classes (upper, middle, lower) who have not previously gambled, may decide to do so when they suddenly lose part of their wealth. . . . And the contrary: gamblers may suddenly stop gambling or gamble less if they win a big prize (1985, pp. 57–58)." Furthermore, for given nominal levels of wealth, larger households will be poorer (per capita) than those with fewer dependents, and, other things equal, older individuals will feel poorer than younger individuals with the same nominal economic status because the orthodox means of acquiring wealth diminish as a function of age. Thus one would expect to find gambling propensities to be greater among household members with large families, and among older individuals. In essence, Brenner argues that "people's attitudes toward risks are affected by their relative positions in the distribution of wealth, and not because they have different 'tastes' " (Brenner, 1985, p. 6).

If gambling is undertaken primarily for its entertainment value rather than as a means to achieve higher levels of wealth, then it can be analyzed in much the same manner as any other discretionary commodity. The consumer allocates time and money to the gambling activity, and implicitly acknowledges the price, in terms of foregone resources, that will ultimately be paid. The variability of winnings and losses remains an integral part of the activity, but the financial motive is secondary to other motives, such as recreation, socialization, exercise of intellectual prowess, or escapism (Rosecrance, 1986).

Certain types of gambling opportunities lend themselves more strongly toward either the entertainment motive or the wealth motive. Lotteries which have low intrinsic entertainment value but very large prizes relative to the cost of participation are the ideal wealth motive gambles. Fixed odds games with even money pay-offs, on the other hand, are more likely to attract entertainment motivated players than wealth seekers. Certain wagers whose expected values can be influenced by the analytical skills of the gambler, such as horse race betting, sports betting, poker, and blackjack, might appeal to both motivations. For example, the challenge of attempting to generate winnings through applications of intellectual skills can be quite rewarding to an individual, independent of the financial outcome of the wagers. However, as a gambler perceives himself more as a professional, and decides to become more committed in terms of time allocation and dependence on winnings as an income source, the wealth motivation may take on greater significance (Hayano, 1984).

Consistent with the arguments of Brenner, there are some individuals who, if they gamble, are more likely to be motivated by the consumption aspects rather than the investment aspects of the activity. Those individuals who are wealthier, younger, or from smaller households, are more likely to view gambling as a commodity rather than as a means to acquiring greater wealth. In similar fashion, persons who are better educated (and therefore have greater wealth acquisition potential through orthodox channels), more secure in their employment and income situations, or have recently experienced significant increases in their wealth, are more likely to view gambling from the entertainment motive than from the wealth motive.

GAMBLING AND RATIONALITY

The economic models of consumer behavior are all based on the premise that self-interested and goal-oriented behavior will result in consumption patterns that fulfill the best interests of the consumer. Gambling poses some challenges to that view because of the fact that, at least for problem or pathological gamblers, gambling patterns are often self-destructive, and the behavior manifested is clearly irrational (illogical) in linking goals to expenditure patterns. Even for "normal" gamblers, over-indulgence in the form of losing more than initially planned at the gaming activities is not an unusual occurrence.

The issue of over-spending on gambling activities by rational economic gamblers was addressed by Eadington for destination casino resorts (1975, pp. 57–69). Such individuals, who probably (though not necessarily) gamble because of the entertainment motive, initially allocate time and money to "casino visits" away from their places of residence. Budgets are determined by expectations of gambling losses. If the gambler does not lose as much as was initially expected, then more money-intensive activities, either gambling or nongambling, are pursued; greater expenditures than initially planned are actually made. On the other hand, if the gambler loses more than expected, there is a strong temptation to introduce new money into the situation (i.e. enlarging the financial budget for the trip) because of the already incurred fixed costs of the visit, and the relatively high value placed on the remaining time at the casino. This asymmetry implies that, on average, gamblers at a destination resort will spend and lose more than they had originally planned.

Some irrationalities in gambling have been noted by earlier economists. Adam Smith argued that "the chance of gain is by every man more or less overvalued, and the chance of loss is by most men undervalued and by scarce any man who is in tolerable health and spirits, valued more than its worth." For it is "the overweening conceit which the greater part of men have of their own abilities" that leads them to miscalculate the true probabilities of winning in their gambling ventures (Smith, 1776, p. 107). Support for Smith's findings can be found in the body of recent literature on horse racing that points out that favorites tend to be undersubscribed by bettors, and longshots are oversubscribed, implying that bettors are overestimating the probabilities of winning on longshot prospects (See, for example, Snyder, 1978).

Another angle on the irrationality of gambling examines the relationship between gambling, superstition, and the understanding of how the external environment works. Thorstein Veblen argued that gambling makes workers "stupid" in the sense that they try to impute causality to what are truly chance events in gambling games, and then they carry these superstitions into the workplace and have greater difficulty understanding the cause-effect relationships that govern production. "Through its cumulative effect upon the habitual attitude of the population, even a slight or inconspicuous bias towards accounting for every day facts by recourse to other ground than that of quantitative causation may work an appreciable lowering of the collective industrial efficiency of a community" (Veblen, 1899).

RATIONALITY AND PUBLIC POLICY

For policy questions dealing with gambling, issues of consumer rationality are of considerable importance. The following arguments represent the extreme positions that could be taken. Suppose one of society's major premises is freedom of choice over one's actions, as long as individual choices do not interfere with the rights of other members of society. Suppose further that the great majority of gamblers are rational and logical individuals, and that gambling creates few negative externalities in society (such as theft, family dissolution, suicide, etc.). It then becomes difficult to support prohibitions against some or all gambling behavior regardless of the motivations of the participants. To do so could only be justified in the context of attempting to impose the value system of one group in society on society at large, i.e. gambling should be prohibited because it is immoral.

On the other hand, suppose a large proportion of gamblers in society could be classified as pathological. One interpretation of their behavior is that it is not dictated by choice but rather by compulsion, and without choice, there is no economic rationality. In this case, gambling losses by pathological gamblers would reflect unwitting transfers from gamblers to the suppliers of gambling services. Instead of creating benefits for both buyers and sellers (which is the result of free and, by definition, mutually advantageous trade among willing rational parties), such transactions would be clearly exploitative, where the suppliers of gambling services would be extracting the wealth of pathological gamblers, an income transfer with no clear benefits to society. Because of the absence of "free choice" on the part of the gamblers, the legitimacy of the income transfers (the gambling losses) would come under question in a property rights context. Under these circumstances, a strong case could be made in favor of prohibiting some or all forms of gambling (Eadington, 1982).

The case for legalization of gambling is often based on the argument that people are, in the main, rational, and they should be allowed to spend their wealth in any manner that they see fit, and that the state has no right to interfere in those decisions. For wealth motivated gamblers, who would tend to come from relatively poorer classes in society, the same case can be made, even though increased gambling by the poor would actually lead to greater distortions in the distribution of income. Brenner argues: "The facts seem to indicate that people know very well that the odds are against them, yet they also know that through gambling they have a chance to become rich, that is, to change significantly their position in the distribution of wealth . . . at the slight expense of the price of a lottery ticket. Restricting gambling therefore imposes a tax on the hopes and dreams of the relatively poor" (1985, p. 11).

The resolution of which policies toward gambling the state should adopt depends largely on the following questions: what proportion of gamblers in society are pathological, and can their problems be mitigated in ways that do not restrict the rights of participation in gambling activities by normal gamblers. In summary, the pathological gambler, who often exhibits the same emotional immaturity as a child, ought to be treated by society in a paternalistic manner, whereas a normal gambler, who has reached majority, should be treated as an adult. If clear measures could be devised for determining the proportions of normal versus pathological gamblers in society, and then for establishing methods of separating the normal from the pathological, public policies dealing with gambling would be much easier to formulate. Regrettably, we are still a long way from those objectives.

REFERENCES

Brenner, R. (1983). *History — The human gamble*. Chicago: The University of Chicago Press.
Brenner, R. (1985). *Betting on ideas*. Chicago: The University of Chicago Press.
Eadington, W.R. (1973). *The economics of gambling behavior: A Qualitative Study of Nevada's Gambling Industry*. Reno: University of Nevada Bureau of Business and Economic Research.
Eadington, W.R. (1975). Economic implications of legalized casino gambling, *Journal of Behavioral*

Economics, 4, (1).
Eadington, W.R. (1982). Regulatory objectives and the expansion of casino gambling, *Nevada Review of Business and Economics,* Fall, 4–13.
Friedman, M. & Savage, L.J. (1948). The utility analysis of choices involving risk. *Journal of Political Economy, 56,* 279–304.
Hardy, O. (1923). *Risk and risk bearing.* Chicago: The University of Chicago Press.
Hayano, D. (July, 1974). The professional gambler: fame, fortune and failure. *The Annals of the American Academy of Political and Social Science, 474,* 157–167.
Henderson, J.M. and Richard E. Quandt (1980). *Micro-Economic Theory: A Mathematical Approach.* New York: McGraw-Hill.
Ignatin, G. & Smith, R.F. (1976). The economics of gambling. In W.R. Eadington (ed.), *Gambling and society.* Springfield, Illinois: Charles C. Thomas Publisher.
Marshall, A. (1930). *Principles of economics,* eighth edition. London: McMillan.
Rosecrance, J. (1986). The sociology of casino gamblers. *Nevada Public Affairs Review, 2,* 27–31.
Smith, A. (1776). *The wealth of nations.* New York: Modern Library Edition (1937).
Snyder, W.W. (Sept., 1978). Horse racing: testing the efficient markets model. *Journal of Finance, 33,* 1109–1118.
Tec, N. (1964). *Gambling in Sweden.* Totowa, New Jersey: Bedminster Press.
Tsukahara, T. & Brumm, H.J. (1976). Economic rationality, psychology, and decision-making under uncertainty. In W.R. Eadington (ed.), *Gambling and society.* Springfield, Illinois: Charles C. Thomas Publisher, pp. 92–107.
Veblen, T. (1899). The belief in luck, from *The theory of the leisure class.* In R. Herman (ed.) (1967) *Gambling.* New York: Harper & Row, pp. 107–112.

Physiological Factors as Determinants of Pathological Gambling

Peter L. Carlton and Paul Manowitz
Department of Psychiatry UMDNJ — Robert Wood Johnson Medical School

Analyses of the etiology of pathological gambling have tended to emphasize psychosocial factors. Although these factors are undoubtedly of major significance in determining ultimate behavioral outcome, an emphasis on them should not obscure the possible role of other, biologically based determinants that may interact with the psychosocial. The plausibility of just such an interactive view is examined here by exploring specific biochemical hypotheses, their testability and their implications.

INTRODUCTION

How are we to conceive of the etiology of pathological gambling? The answer to that question is crucial because it determines the research

---

The research reported here and the preparation of the paper itself were supported by a grant from the New Jersey Lottery Commission; we are indebted to Ms. Denise Lantz and to Ms. Lu-Ann Fine for their assistance. We are also indebted to Drs. Leonide Goldstein and Marshall Swartzburg for valuable discussions of the manuscript.

Many of the ideas elaborated here were first discussed at the University of Medicine and Dentistry of New Jersey Symposium on Compulsive Gambling, 1982, and at the Symposium on Pathological Gambling sponsored by the Carrier Foundation, 1983.

Send reprint requests to: Peter L. Carlton, Ph.D., Department of Psychiatry, UMDNJ — Robert Wood Johnson Medical School, Piscataway, New Jersey, 08854.

strategy that one adopts in attempting to understand pathological gambling.

One answer to the question about the etiology of pathological gambling focuses on psychosocial factors because it is clear that pathological gamblers can be characterized in terms of particular psychosocial histories. That characterization does not, however, directly address yet another question: Why is it that some persons with a characteristic psychosocial history do become pathological gamblers, whereas most persons with the same history do not? For example, pathological gamblers may have been abused as children, may have been raised in single parent homes, and may have suffered from a variety of other disruptions, but so too have many who do not become pathological in their adult gambling behavior. It may be, of course, that a disruptive psychosocial history produces only a generalized tendency to pathology; the action of additional environmental factors may be required if particular pathology is to develop, if it develops at all.

There is, in addition, yet another view of etiology: The prospect that *biologically* based predispositions interact with psychosocial history and other environmental factors to determine ultimate behavioral outcome. Such an interactive view has certainly enhanced our understanding of alcoholism. Whether it will also prove to be useful in our understanding of pathological gambling is an issue that is yet to be explored.

In considering the potential utility of such an interactive view, it is important to recognize that a focus on biological factors does not imply that psychosocial and environmental factors are not of crucial importance. Indeed, such a focus is entirely a matter of conceptual convenience; pathological gambling (or any other disorder) surely cannot be understood in the absence of a consideration of the role of factors other than the biological. Furthermore, it is certain that biological determinants will be of greater significance in some persons, whereas other factors will be of greater significance in others. A brief consideration of a disorder wholly unrelated to pathological gambling will amplify the point.

High levels of cholesterol in the blood (hypercholesterolemia) can be a significant factor in coronary heart disease. Levels of cholesterol are, of course, determined by diet and diet is partly determined by psychosocial history (e.g., past eating habits, culturally based tastes and aversions). But diet is also determined by current environmental factors (e.g., availability of certain foods, familial and peer pressures). In addition, it is clear that a biological predisposition interacts with these factors; in some patients, the hypercholesterolemia is directly determined by a genetic fault, whereas there is only a less direct, familial pattern in others. Thus, biological factors, in varying degrees, interact with psychosocial and environmental factors in determining the level of cholesterol and, thereby, coronary heart disease.

But, given all that, how are we to determine whether the elucidation of biological determinants is likely to enhance our understanding of pathological gambling itself? The final answer to that question can only be given when the relevant research has been done. We can, however, ask another, preliminary question: Is it realistic to suppose that we can, in fact, ever determine whether biological predispositions have a role in the etiology of pathological gambling? That question, in turn, relates to four others: First, do we have information about brain function that is sufficient to generate ideas about such predispositions; second, are these ideas plausible ones when viewed concretely (i.e., are they more than mere "pie in the sky"); third, do these ideas also have more than plausibility (i.e., do they generate directly testable expectations); fourth, do these expectations, if confirmed, have clear implications for treatment?

We hope to show that the answers to all four of these questions are positive ones; in the process of discussing them, we also hope to show that it is indeed reasonable to suppose that we can ultimately elucidate the biological factors that contribute to the etiology of pathological gambling.

ELECTROENCEPHALOGRAPHIC STUDIES OF PATHOLOGICAL GAMBLERS

We began to address our question about biological predispositions by studying a "brain-based" measure that has been shown to be useful in discriminating among various clinical entities (see Goldstein, 1983). In particular, we studied the so-called "brain waves" that are obtained from electroencephalographic (EEG) recordings.

It is well established that such EEG recordings show characteristic patterns in response to particular task requirements. Specifically, verbal-sequential tasks lead to a greater activation of the left hemisphere of the brain (relative to the right hemisphere), whereas nonverbal-spatial tasks generate a complementary activation pattern (i.e., greater activation of the right hemisphere relative to the left). Given all that, our basic question was this: Could these different EEG patterns be used to discriminate recovered pathological gamblers from matched controls?

As it turned out, the answer to that question was a positive one. That is, pathological gamblers showed deficits in the degree of EEG differentiation produced by simple verbal *vs.* nonverbal tasks. Put another way, the brain of the recovered pathological gambler is apparently less able to respond differentially to different task requirements. (These experiments have been briefly described by Goldstein, *et al.*, 1985, and discussed in detail by Carlton and Goldstein, 1987).

It is important to recognize that the EEG deficits that we obtained were extremely subtle ones, detectable only by sophisticated computer analysis. Such subtlety is to be expected in that all subjects were functioning at a high level of social adjustment (e.g., typically they were married, had children, owned a suburban home, two cars and earned substantial annual incomes); we are not dealing with a pronounced neurological deficit. Furthermore, the gamblers we studied had all been abstinent for at least two years. It is thus an open question whether active gamblers, while actually gambling, would also show the activation deficits we obtained.

Still another question about these EEG deficits is the extent to which they are unique to pathological gamblers. The fact of the matter is that they are not. Indeed, parallel deficits have been obtained from, among other groups, children with Attention Deficit Disorder (A.D.D.; see Carlton and Goldstein, 1987).

This finding is hardly a surprising one. That is, effective attention must be based on the brain making effective discriminations of the requirements of different tasks; thus, defective attention (as in A.D.D. children) can reasonably be expected to be reflected in EEG recordings of the kind we are considering here. More pertinent, however, is the parallelism of EEG findings in pathological gamblers and A.D.D. children. That parallelism raises an obvious question: Is there a tendency for pathological gamblers to have also been A.D.D. children?

A positive answer to that question would bear directly on some of the issues we have already discussed. In particular, if pathological gambling is related to A.D.D., then our finding of EEG deficits in adult gamblers would suggest that some of the characteristics of A.D.D. were "carried forward" into adulthood. The EEG deficit would thus reflect an abiding trait and, therefore, a general characteristic of the pathological gambler that is presumably unique to neither recovery nor to a particular environmental setting. Accordingly, it was important that we obtain information about the A.D.D.-related behaviors that may have characterized the pathological gambler as a child.

A.D.D. AND PATHOLOGICAL GAMBLING

In order to obtain information about A.D.D.-related behaviors during childhood, it is necessary to use retrospective questionnaires. Unfortunately, such questionnaires are severely limited in their usefulness. They may be biased by present circumstances, by faulty memory and by a vividness of past behavior that has been artifactually amplified by repeated family stories (e.g., "You always were such an active kid"). Be that as it may, it is very unlikely that retrospective reports arise from a *total* behavioral vacuum; it is therefore most reasonable to suppose that differences obtained from such reports do truly reflect qualitative behavioral differences, even though the quantitative aspects of these differences may be substantially distorted.

Our use of a retrospective questionnaire involved a list of statements about childhood behavior (e.g., "When I was a child, I was nervous;" see Carlton and Goldstein, 1987, for further details). Each of these statements was rated by recovered gamblers and by matched controls. As it turned out, the average rating assigned by gamblers to A.D.D. items was substantially higher than that assigned by controls; i.e., there was clear evidence pointing to a greater frequency of A.D.D.-related behaviors during the childhood of the pathological gambler.

These findings generate at least two significant conclusions: First, as we have already noted, the indication that gamblers were A.D.D. children, when taken in conjunction with their adult EEG deficits, implies that they have continued to have at least a residual form of A.D.D. That first conclusion leads directly to the second: Some alcoholics have also been shown to have been A.D.D. children and to have a residual form of the disorder in adulthood (Wender, Reimherr & Wood, 1981; DeObaldia, Parsons & Yohman, 1983; Tarter *et al.,* 1977; Wood, Wender & Reimherr, 1983). Thus, taken together, our data suggest that A.D.D. may be a trait characteristic of both pathological gamblers and alcoholics.

PETER L. CARLTON AND PAUL MANOWITZ

PATHOLOGICAL GAMBLERS AND ALCOHOLICS

Our conclusion about the similarity of pathological gamblers and alcoholics *vis-a-vis* A.D.D. was entirely circumstantial because, at the time we drew it, we had not ourselves directly compared the two groups. Accordingly, we again administered our questionnaire in a second study that is still in progress.

Once again, gamblers tended to assign A.D.D. items a higher rating, whereas controls again assigned them a relatively low rating. More to the point, recovered alcoholics rated the A.D.D. items at a high average level almost identical to that assigned by pathological gamblers. This result thus directly confirms expectation based on our earlier study. Furthermore, this confirmation is pertinent to a potentially significant conjecture about the role of biologically based determining factors in both alcoholism and pathological gambling. We will discuss that conjecture in the following sections.

DETERMINING FACTORS: THE ROLE OF INHIBITION

The finding that alcoholics and pathological gamblers share certain characteristics leads to the conjecture that they may also share common etiological determinants. (It may also turn out that other disorders of impulse control like overeating and drug abuse also share these same etiological factors.) But, if that is so, what might these factors be? Answering that question requires a more detailed consideration of A.D.D. itself.

A deficit in attention cannot be related in any obvious way to either excessive gambling or excessive alcohol intake. However, the diagnosis of A.D.D. is based on another behavioral characteristic in addition to the relative inability to sustain attention. This second characteristic is labeled as impulsivity: The tendency to respond impetuously, apparently without forethought; the relative inability to delay gratification (reward); the tendency to respond even if the consequence of such responding may be negative (punishing).

The term impulsivity implies a deficit in inhibition, an inability to "hold back." And, so too, does an attention deficit imply a deficit in inhibition, because to "focus" attention requires an *in*attention to other, competing stimuli that must be functionally filtered if they are not to disrupt the attentional process itself. Thus, both an attention deficit and impulsivity have a common property: Both can be related to deficits in inhibitory processes.

This concept relates, in turn, to the idea that alcoholics and pathological gamblers may share an inhibitory deficit that leads to deficits in the ability to "self-limit" their behavior. It is, then, the relative inability to "cut-off" certain ongoing behaviors that leads to pathology. Furthermore, the pathology in question may take the form of gambling or alcoholism and may turn out, as we have noted, to include drug abuse as well as overeating.

That conceptualization generates three questions: If we are considering a basic inhibitory deficit, then (1) what physiological factors may determine that deficit, (2) how might such factors be analyzed and (3) what factors determine the link to specific forms of pathology? We will briefly consider each of these questions below.

DETERMINING FACTORS: BRAIN SEROTONIN (5-HT) AND INHIBITION

A biologically based predisposing factor of the kind we are discussing will inevitably be expressed in terms of brain biochemistry because it is the biochemistry of the brain that ultimately controls its activity. Accordingly, we can ask: What normally active neurochemicals might be related to such inhibitory deficits?

In asking that question we are implicitly asking another: Does a reduction in the normal activity of some neurochemical lead to a lack of inhibition? As it happens, a positive answer to that question is close at hand: A very large number of studies directly implicate a naturally occurring substance in just such an inhibitory role. This substance is called serotonin; it is also called 5-hydroxytryptamine (5-HT).

In laboratory animals, it is possible to experimentally reduce 5-HT activity in the brain by the use of drugs or by inducing brain lesions. When that is done, dramatic increases in reactivity occur in an enormously wide variety of situations (Weissman, 1973; Harvey & Yunger, 1973; Carlton & Advokat, 1973). The animal behaves as if environmental input is relatively unrestrained by collateral inhibition. As a result, the tendency to respond is massively increased and may, because respond-

PETER L. CARLTON AND PAUL MANOWITZ

ing necessarily precludes sleep, even lead to sleeplessness.

There is also, in addition to the use of drugs or brain lesions, another way to reduce brain 5-HT. The body manufactures 5-HT from an essential amino acid that is in the diet. This amino acid is called tryptophan (TRP) and, because it is required for the production of 5-HT, reduced TRP leads to reduced 5-HT in brain. It is not surprising, therefore, that reduced dietary intake of TRP can also produce many features of the array of effects due to reducing 5-HT by other means (Lytle et al. 1975; Gibbons et al. 1979; Gibbons et al. 1981; Walters, Davis & Sheard, 1979).

More to the point, it is of particular interest that reduced dietary TRP reduces attentional processes in humans, at least in some circumstances (Young et al. 1985). One obvious interpretation of this finding is that reducing TRP reduces 5-HT in brain and thus reduces the inhibitory mechanism necessary for sustained attention. Furthermore, other disorders of impulse control associated with suicide and/or aggression are also characterized by low levels of 5-HT metabolites in brain (Goodwin & Post, 1983). Impulsivity is again clearly related to 5-HT deficits.

It is also possible to turn these relationships on their head and study the effects of increased rather than decreased 5-HT function. In laboratory animals, increased 5-HT activity due to administration of TRP can reverse the effects of attenuated 5-HT activity; in humans, increased TRP produces sedation (i.e., behavioral hyporeactivity), promotes sleep (Young, 1986) and, most significant, has been reported to reduce some of the signs of A.D.D. (Nemzer et al. 1986).

Taken together, these findings provide a coherent network of interrelated phenomena. But how can this array of findings be specifically related to pathological gambling and to the processes pertinent to that disorder?

DETERMINING FACTORS: ANALYSIS OF SEROTONIN FUNCTION

Our discussion of 5-HT as an inhibitory factor in brain function implies that the pathological gambler can be characterized as having a 5-HT deficit that leads to impulsivity. That implication leads, in turn, to a straightforward experimental test: The pathological gambler should be relatively insensitive to the effects of increased 5-HT function. The gambler should, for example, be relatively insensitive to the sedative effects of increased brain 5-HT due to increased TRP. Furthermore, given the relationship of 5-HT to suicide, it may not be coincidental that pathological gamblers have a suicide rate about 100 times the national average (Custer & Milt, 1985).

An alternative but more circumstantial way of examining the role of 5-HT in the human brain is to study the effects of certain "natural experiments." For example, children with phenylketonuria (PKU), if they are untreated, show relatively low levels of TRP in blood and, not unexpectedly, signs that can be associated with a lack of inhibitory processes (e.g., agitated behavior, hyperactive reflexes and high levels of motor activity; Knox, 1972). The effects of PKU are not, of course, "pure" in that these patients suffer from a variety of other biochemical abnormalities. Thus, the fact that they show deficits attributable to deficits in inhibition can only very circumstantially be related to the deficits in 5-HT function that they also show.

Similar considerations apply to patients suffering from Anorexia Nervosa. These patients eat virtually nothing at all and, as a result, show severe deficits in TRP that presumably lead, in turn, to deficits in brain 5-HT (Coppen et al. 1976). It is an open question whether data obtained from these patients will confirm the presumed relationship of 5-HT to inhibition that we have hypothesized.

A related "natural experiment" is available in actively drinking alcoholics who, like patients with Anorexia Nervosa, show relatively low levels of TRP (Branchey, Shaw & Lieber, 1981) and, presumably, low levels of brain 5-HT. Indeed, this fact suggests a self-amplifying chain reaction in which low initial levels of 5-HT activity increase impulsivity, increased impulsivity increases the likelihood of drinking, drinking itself further reduces 5-HT activity and this reduction further increases the likelihood of continued drinking. Such a conceptualization is at least consonant with the finding that pharamacologically increased 5-HT activity can substantially enhance abstinence in recovering alcoholics (Naranjo, Sellers & Lawrin, 1986).

Incidentally, it is very unlikely that blood levels of TRP and/or 5-HT could be used to differentiate pathological gamblers—or, for that matter, A.D.D. children. That is, the very subtle differences in brain 5-HT activity that presumably underlie these pathologies cannot reasonably be expected to be reflected in a peripheral source like blood.

In contrast, untreated PKU children, anorexics and actively drinking alcoholics show such massive dietary disruption that low levels of blood TRP are produced.

DETERMINING FACTORS: IMPLICATIONS FOR TREATMENT

The ideas about physiological predisposition that we have been considering lead directly to an implication for treatment. In fact, such an implication amounts to a second kind of experimental test of the ideas themselves.

The implication is clear: If we can demonstrate a functional deficit in the activity of brain 5-HT, then the next step will be to determine whether increasing 5-HT activity will serve as a useful adjunct to psychotherapeutic interventions involved in treatment. Fortunately, 5-HT can be increased pharmacologically either by oral doses of TRP itself or by the use of other drugs that indirectly increase 5-HT activity.

DETERMINING FACTORS: ENVIRONMENTAL MODULATION OF BEHAVIORAL OUTCOME

The material we have discussed adds up to a persuasive case for the idea that brain 5-HT is involved in pathological gambling as well as alcoholism and, perhaps, drug abuse and overeating. Providing a persuasive case is not, however, equivalent to the direct experimental demonstration of such an involvement; only future research can provide that. But, even if the role of 5-HT as a determining factor is empirically confirmed, the question of how that factor eventuates in particular behaviors will remain unanswered. As we have already suggested, even if a deficit in the activity of brain 5-HT is unequivocally shown to be a predisposing factor, two clear questions will remain: First, because such a predisposition will not irrevocably lead to pathological gambling (or alcoholism or overeating or drug abuse), it will be necessary to determine why some individuals "escape" their predisposition and fail to develop any pathology at all; second, because some predisposed individuals develop certain pathologies and other individuals develop other pathologies, it will be necessary to determine why different individuals "choose" different pathologies. Thus, the fine-grained analysis of psychosocial history, environmental factors and the details of personality structure will be required if we are to fully understand these disorders. Understanding "biology" alone will surely not suffice.

REFERENCES

Branchey, L., Shaw, S., and Lieber, C.S. (1981). Ethanol impairs tryptophan transport into the brain and depresses serotonin. *Life Sciences, 29,* 2751-2755.
Carlton, P.L., and Advokat, C. (1973). Attenuated habituation due to parachlorophenylalanine. *Pharmacology Biochemistry and Behavior, 1,* 657-663.
Carlton, P.L., and Goldstein, L. (1987). Physiological determinants of pathological gambling. In T. Galski (Ed.), *A handbook of pathological gambling.* Springfield, IL: Charles C. Thomas.
Coppen, A.J., Gupta, R.K., Eccleston, E.G., Wood, K.M., Wakeling, A., and de Sousa, V.F.A. (1976). Plasma-tryptophan in anorexia nervosa. *Lancet,* 961.
Custer, R. and Milt, H. (1985). *When luck runs out: Help for compulsive gamblers and their families.* New York: Facts on File.
DeObaldia, R., Parsons, O.A., and Yohman, R. (1983). Minimal brain dysfunction symptoms claimed by primary and secondary alcoholics: Relation to cognitive functioning. *International Journal of Neuroscience, 20,* 173-182.
Gibbons, J.L., Barr, G.A., Bridger, W.H., and Leibowitz, S.F. (1979). Manipulations of dietary tryptophan: Effects on mouse killing and brain serotonin in the rat. *Brain Research, 169,* 139-151.
Gibbons, J.L., Barr, G.A., Bridger, W.H., and Leibowtiz, S.F. (1981). L-tryptophan's effects on mouse killing, feeding, drinking, locomotion, and brain serotonin. *Pharmacology Biochemistry & Behavior, 15,* 201-206.
Goldstein, L. (1983). Some EEG correlates of behavioral states and traits in humans. *Research Communications in Psychology, Psychiatry and Behavior, 8,* 115-141.
Goldstein, L., Manowitz, P., Nora, R., Swartzburg, M., and Carlton, P.L. (1985). Differential EEG activation and pathological gambling. *Biological Psychiatry, 20,* 1232-1234.
Goodwin, F.K., and Post, R.M. (1983). 5-Hydroxytryptamine and depression: A model for the interaction of normal variance with pathology. *British Journal of Clinical Pharmacology, 15,* 393S-405S.
Harvey, J.A. and Yunger, L.M. (1973). Relationship between telecephalic content of serotonin and pain sensitivity. In J. Barchas & E. Usdin (Eds.), *Serotonin and behavior* (pp. 179-189). New York: Academic.
Knox, W.E. (1972). Phenylketonuria. In J.B. Stanbury, J.B. Wyngaarden and D.S. Fredrickson (eds.), *The metabolic basis of inherited disease.* New York: McGraw-Hill.
Lytle, L.D., Messing, R.B., Fisher, L., and Phebus, L. (1975). Effects of long-term corn consumption on brain serotonin and the response to electric shock. *Science, 190,* 692-694.
Naranjo. C.A., Sellers, E.M., and Lawrin, M.O. (1986). Modulation of ethanol intake by serotonin uptake inhibitors. *Journal of Clinical Psychiatry, 47,* 16-22.
Nemzer, E.D., Arnold, L.E., Votolato, N.A., and McConnell, H. (1986). Amino acid supplementation as therapy for attention deficit disorder. *Journal of the American Academy of Child Psychiatry, 25,* 509-513.
Tarter, R.E., McBride, H., Buonpane, H., and Schneider, D.U. (1977). Differentiation of alcoholics: Childhood history of minimal brain dysfunction, family history and drinking pattern. *Archives of General Psychiatry, 34,* 761-768.
Walters, J.K., Davis, M., and Sheard, M.H. (1979). Tryptophan-free diet: Effects on the acoustic startle reflex in rats. *Psychopharmacology, 62,* 103-109.
Weissman, A. (1973). Behavioral pharmacology of p-chlorophenylalanine (PCPA). In J. Barchas and E. Usdin (eds.), *Serotonin and behavior* (pp. 235-248). New York: Academic.

Wender, P.H., Reimherr, F.W., and Wood, D.R. (1981). Attention deficit disorder (minimal brain dysfunction) in adults. *Archives of General Psychiatry, 38,* 449-456.

Wood, D., Wender, P.H., and Reimherr, F.W. (1983). The prevalence of attention deficit disorder, residual type, or minimal brain dysfunction, in a population of male alcoholic patients. *American Journal of Psychiatry, 140,* 95-98.

Young, S.N. (1986). The clinical psychopharmacology of tryptophan. In R.J. Wurtman and J.J. Wurtman (eds.), *Nutrition and the brain* (Vol. 7, pp. 49-88). New York: Raven.

Young, S.N., Smith, S.E., Pihl, R.O., and Ervin, F.R. (1985). Tryptophan depletion causes a rapid lowering of mood in normal males. *Psychopharmacology, 87,* 173-177.

Book Review of
COMPULSIVE GAMBLERS[1]

Mark G. Dickerson
London: Longman Press, 1984, 150 pp.

As part of the Longman Applied Psychology series devoted to concise texts on current topics in psychology, Mark G. Dickerson has succeeded in creating a volume which provides a wide range of valuable information appropriate for both the professional and the interested general reader alike. The scope of the text is broad covering the history of gambling, theories on gambling, its epidemiology and demographics, and how compulsive gamblers can gain control over their behavior.

Following a brief history of gambling, Dickerson reviews sociological and psychological explanations for gambling behavior. These explanations include personality differences, decision theory, and such lesser known, but useful, sociological concepts such as Callois' (1962) principles of *agon* (competitive games) and *alea* (games of chance) used to describe how societies perceive the achievement of personal advancements.

In a chapter titled "Who are they and how do they gamble" the author summarizes research on demographic and personality characteristics of gamblers, and examines their games, their subjective experiences

---

Send reprint requests to: Martin Chaplin, M.A., Department of Psychology, University of Missouri-St. Louis, 8001 Natural Bridge Road, St. Louis, MO 63121.

[1]Not yet published in the U.S. For purchasing information write: Longman Group Ltd., Longman House, Burnt Hill, Marlow, Essex CM20 2JE England.

when gambling, and how gamblers actually regain control or stop gambling. The latter topic, which includes Custer's (1982) phases of recovery, would have been more appropriate in the chapter devoted to the recovery process. This chapter also includes information on the costs of gambling to society and the manifold problems facing the compulsive gambler including legal, financial, employment, and interpersonal problems.

Chapter five seeks to answer the puzzling question: "Why do they persist when losing?" Unfortunately, Dickerson devotes much of the chapter to definitions of "pathological gambling" and not to answering the question at hand. Some of the most interesting and insightful reading occurs here with the examination of the well-known (to gamblers and clinicians) but little understood phenomenon of "chasing."

The last two chapters are devoted to the theoretical and practical aspects of how gamblers may abstain or return to controlled gambling. Dickerson does not take a side on the controversy regarding abstinence versus controlled gambling as the proper goal of treatment but attempts to shed light on both goals. Perhaps the most valuable part of the text is the last chapter devoted to a revised and expanded version of Dickerson's self-help handbook for compulsive gamblers first published in 1975. This version is an extensive and practical plan and includes most of the recovery mechanisms espoused by Gamblers Anonymous and others (e.g., Custer, 1982). These seven pages should be required reading for all mental health professionals and especially those unsure how to treat a gambling problem.

Overall, the text is a thorough and brief review of the important aspects of compulsive gambling with information for a wide audience. At the end of each of the seven chapters Dickerson has a summary which nicely pulls together the diverse topics discussed. The concepts and theories mentioned are well referenced which will allow readers to obtain more information readily. There are some minor flaws. The organization of the topics in the chapters is clumsy at times with some topics better suited for inclusion in other chapters. While Dickerson claims to have an atheoretical stance, he reveals a distaste for psychoanalytic and aversion techniques and a strong preference for cognitive-behavioral approaches. Dickerson might have included one or two case studies of compulsive gamblers which would have provided a feel for the subject not possible with only the theoretical and research data. This last consideration is not necessarily a flaw but may reflect a proper decision by the author to limit the scope of his work.

Martin Chaplin, M.A.
University of Missouri-St. Louis.

REFERENCES

Callois, R. (1962). *Man, play, and games.* London: Thames & Hudson.
Custer, R.L. (1982). Pathological gambling. In Whitfield, A. (Ed.), *Patients with alcoholism and other drug problems.* New York: Yearbook Publishers.

Book Review of
THE CHASE: CAREER OF THE COMPULSIVE GAMBLER

by **Henry R. Lesieur**
Schenkman Publishing Co. Cambridge, Mass. 1984.

The body of book-length literature on pathological gambling is small. Many of the works have quickly gone out of print, and it is rare that a second edition appears. The availability of Henry Lesieur's *The Chase* in a new edition is perhaps the best testimony to its usefulness to those who desire a description of the events in life which lead to a career of compulsive gambling.

The major difference between the 1977 edition and the present one

---

Send reprint requests to: Terry J. Knapp, Ph.D., Department of Psychology, University of Nevada-Las Vegas, Las Vegas, Nevada 89154.

is the change in perspective of the author. During the ensuing years, he was transformed "from someone who disbelieves in the medical model to one who now endorses it" (with some reservations). He has come to recognize, mainly through his contact with the National Council on Compulsive Gambling, that "the medical model has helped hundreds if not thousands of gamblers. Even if they are not 'sick' in the philosophical sense of the term, calling them sick makes sense when it comes to attempting to alter their destructive behavior pattern."

A sociologist who comes to adopt a "medical model" is an object of interest to those who study general social theory, and who may have only a passing interest in the particular topic of compulsive gambling. In this regard, *The Chase* may be read to gain a perspective on what our culture is willing to regard as an "addiction," and for an understanding of the kinds of reasons that a "social" oriented theorist would begin to accept a "medically" oriented model of deviant behavior.

The "Afterword," titled "Sociologists and the Medical Model of Pathological Gambling," and the first appendix, which concerns a detailed account of the research process, help to explain why the author has changed his views. Some of the details in the research section may appear mundane but as one who has used tape recordings in his research, I found the suggestions in this regard very helpful.

The readers of this journal, however, are undoubtedly interested in *The Chase* for whatever enlightenment it might provide on gambling. I would single out several important points:

- The use of "career" to characterize the development of pathological gambling. Too often in the psychological and psychiatric literature compulsive gambling is discussed as excessive behavior in isolated episodes. Such discussions miss much of what is contributed by the developmental perspective of the "career" model.
- The use of the metaphor a "spiral of options" to identify the particular pattern of behavior associated with the developing career of a pathological gambler. This metaphor serves to focus our attention away from any specific bet or wager to the dysfunctional pattern that distinguishes the pathological from the social or professional gambler.
- Finally, the metaphor of "Chase," or "Putting good money after bad," to capture the specific daily behaviors that lead to

pathological gambling. The opening sentence to the chapter on "The Chase" warrants quotation, "The 'Chase' begins when a gambler bets either to pay everyday bills that are due, or to 'get even' from a fall. A gambler can chase on a short-term or a long-term basis. Those locked into the long-term chase are compulsive gamblers."

It would be useful for those skilled in formal analysis to develop a quantitative model to reflect the descriptive accounts given to support this definition of the chase. What are the particular contingencies, or individual personality differences that lead some persons to be "locked" in a career of decreasing options for obtaining good money to chase bad money?

Much of the rest of the book is concerned with describing the relationship between the "Chase" and the consequence it has on the family, marriage, vocation and business, and its direct connection to the commission of crimes. The model suggested is an interactive one, in which the potential therapeutic benefits of employment and marriage in inhibiting gambling are also discussed.

The seven contingencies which the author believes lead to the "shape" of the spiral in any particular case of compulsive gambling provide a useful model for future quantitative studies, or attempts to measure and directly assess the impact of each of these contingencies. A schematic or diagram would have helped the reader to keep the contingencies more in focus.

References added since the first edition are listed separately following the new afterword. This is a useful feature when one is interested in only the new material, but it means that a user unfamiliar with the first edition must remember to look in two places for a complete set of references.

I suppose a psychologist reading the work of a sociologist is likely to feel that too much of the "psychological literature" has been neglected. I do. There is, however, a pointed discussion of the DSM-III criteria for pathological gambling, as well as some suggestions for future research.

The Chase provides one of the best narratives of the life patterns of pathological gamblers, a useful model for describing and, to some degree, explaining their behavior, and a provocative text for debating the issue of medical versus social models. It will serve well in the classroom, and should be read by clinicians contemplating working with pathological gamblers.

Terry J. Knapp, Ph.D.
Dept. of Psychology
University of Nevada-Las Vegas

Book Review of
THINKING BIG, THE EDUCATION OF A GAMBLER

Sol Fox
New York: Atheneum, 1985. $15.95.

This book is a personal account of Sol Fox's sixteen-year experience as a dependent race track gambler. Through a first person narrative, he walks the reader through experiences from his childhood, particularly the loss of his father through divorce, which may have influenced his later gambling behavior. This self analysis then leads into a long, and at times too detailed review of his gambling history and the resulting negative personal financial consequences.

Fox begins by presenting his personal frame of reference with only minimal reference to broader historical, sociological, psychological or public policy perspectives. He then describes his commitment to action and gambling, where he learned how the bookie system worked and how to become more elaborate in his deceptions. Following a period of enforced time out during his military service and as a prisoner of war, he reviews his subsequent 14 plus years of intermittant, excessive gam-

---

Send reprint requests to: Charles D. Maurer, Ph.D., 1001 Broadway, Suite 315, Seattle, Washington 98122.

bling, and finally his eventual withdrawal from pathological gambling. The reader is given brief insights into how he stopped gambling and of his few gambling experiences since decreasing from a compulsive level. These descriptions are quite helpful, given that we hear little about gamblers who change their level of play. The most powerful and engaging chapter in the book is the first. It provides us with an excellent description of his arousal and defeat one spring day at Jamaica racetrack. The remaining narrative is less engaging.

The author makes some attempt to weave in perspectives other than his own experience. There are, however, no footnotes, references, quotes, bibliography, or index. These are major shortcomings that will frustrate even the mildly curious reader. Much of the personal detail is interesting and provides a clear backdrop, but it is tedious. Only the most tenacious reader will persevere. There were, however, some tempting references to the broader topics of his greed, dependence, obsession with eating, and depression that could have easily been expanded.

For the mental health professional the lack of detail on his various change points will be disappointing. For the gambler, the view is so limited that gamblers probably will be disinterested. Most who are currently gambling would never pick up the book; those who have stopped would be disenchanted. So little time is spent on the spouse or family relationships (other than his self-blame and guilt) that most spouses would not learn much new. Those who do read the book will be infuriated by his openly selfish summary. Members of Gamblers Anonymous will find no reference to their groups or other contemporary treatment approaches. Fox's personal analysis with a psychiatrist, apparently unknowledgable about compulsive gambling, may have been more of an influence than he acknowledges. When the psychiatrist dismissed him from treatment (for lack of honesty and effort), the author was left with an unconscious paradox to prove the therapist wrong by stopping gambling or correct by continuing.

The student of compulsive gambling is slowly being exposed to more sources of information, through journal articles, professional papers and proceedings, print media summaries, and autobiographies of gamblers, like *Thinking Big*. There are other autobiographies that are better written, more engaging, and of wider helpfulness. For example, Feodor Dostoyevsky's novelella, *The Gambler* (1866) is one of the first and the finest in this reviewer's opinion. Dostoyevsky's personal dependence on the roulette wheels at the Kurhaus in Wiesbaden is indirectly summarized through his protagonist Alexis. It has been the prompt for a monograph by Sigmund Freud, *Dostoyevsky and Patricide* (1928) and a number of movies.

As the public becomes more curious about the nature of compulsive gambling, there is an explicit need for more contemporary descriptions. William Hoffman, Jr.'s autobiography, *The Loser,* (1966), is a vivid psychological description. Hoffman actively involves the reader in the psychological and social aspects of his gambling dependence. His struggle for action, money, control, and abstinence is engaging, agonizing, moving and tiring. His story ends on the sad but honest revelation of his return to an even deeper level of gambling.

Perhaps the most helpful book, though not autobiographical, is Robert Custer and Harry Milt's *When Luck Runs Out* (1985). In addition to the accurate, clear, and interesting mix of clinical description and real life summaries, it offers educational and pragmatic suggestions to guide the reader. The advantage of Custer and Milt's book over Fox's is in the breadth and depth of knowledge and understanding that is shared. Perhaps, if Fox had collaborated with a mental health professional who understood other facets of his gambling behavior, his book would have generalized his experiences as Custer and Milt's book did.

The value in this book remains that it is one of the few that does describe this misperceived aspect of human behavior. It is candid, open, and revealing. Fox's story offers a positive and hopeful view that individuals can change specific aspects of their behavior and thereby alter the direction of their lives. However, it could have been more enriching had it been broader and more comprehensive.

Charles D. Maurer, Ph.D.
Seattle, Washington

REFERENCES

Dostoyevsky, F. (1966(1866)). *The gambler,* Translated by Jesse Couslon, Middlesex, England; Penguin.

Freud, S. (1952). Dostoyevsky and Patricide. In *Collected papers,* Volume 5, Translated by J. Strachey. London: Haworth Press.

Hoffman, Jr., W. (1966). *The loser,* New York: Funk and Wagnalls.

Custer, R. and Milt, H. (1985). *When Luck Runs Out,* New York: Warner Books.

INDEX

Adcock, Sylvia. *See* Dickerson, Mary.
Anderson, G. and Brown R.I.F.
    Some Applications of Reversal Theory to the Explanations of Gambling and Gambling Addictions   179
Bulme, Sheila B.
    Compulsive Gambling and the Medical Model   238
Brown, R.I.F.
    Dropouts and Continuers in Gamblers Anonymous: Part 2. Analysis of Free-style Accounts of Experiences with GA   68
Brown, R.I.F.
    Pathological Gambling and Associated Patterns of Crime: Comparisons with Alcohol and Other Drug Addictions   98
Brown, R.I.F.
    Dropouts and Continuers in Gamblers Anonymous: Part 3. Some Possible Specific Reasons for Dropout   137
Brown, R.I.F. *See* Anderson, G.
Brown, R.I.F.
    Dropouts and Continuers in Gamblers Anonymous: Part 4. Evaluation and Summary   202
Brown, R.I.F.
    Models of Gambling and Gambling Addictions as Personal Filters   224
Carlton, Peter L. and Manowitz, Paul.
    Physiological Factors as Determinants of Pathological Gambling   275
Chaplin, Martin.
    Compulsive Gamblers by Mark Dickerson   287
Ciarrocchi, Joseph.
    Severity of Impairement in Dually Addicted Gamblers   16
Ciarrocchi, Joseph. *See* Franklin, Joanna.
Corney, William. *See* Cummings, Theodore Wm.
Cummings, Theodore Wm. and Corney, William.

Dickerson, Mark.
    A Conceptual Model of Gambling Behavior: Fishbein's Theory of Reasoned
        Action   190
Dickerson, Mark.
    The Future of Gambling Research: Learning from the Lessons of Alcholism.   249
Dickerson, Mary. and Adcock, Sylvia.
    Mood, Arousal, and Cognitions in Persistant Gambling: Preliminary Investigation of Theoretical Model   3
Eadington, William R.
    Credit Play and Casinos: Profitability, Legitimacy, and Social Responsibility   83
Eadington, William R.
    Economic Perceptions of Gambling Behavior   265
Franklin, Joanna and Ciarrocchi, Joseph.
    The Team Approach: Developing and Experiential Knowledge Base for the Treatment of the Pathological Gambler   60
Heineman, Mary.
    A Comparison: The Treatment of Wives of Alcoholics With the Treatment of Wives of Pathological Gamblers   27
Kaplan, Roy H.
    Lottery Winners: The Myth and Reality   168
Klenow, Daniel J. *See* Lindgren, Elaine H.
Landouceur, Robert. and Mayrand, Marie, Tourigny, Yves.
    Risk Taking Behavior in Gamblers and Non - Gamblers During Prolonged Exposure   115
Lesieur, Henry R. and Puig, Kenneth.
    Insurance Problems and Pathological Gambling   123
Lindgren, Elaine H. and Youngs, George A. Jr., McDonald, Thomas D., Klenow, Daniel J., Schriner, Eldon C.
    The Impact of Gender on Gambling Attitudes and Behavior   155
Manowitz, Paul. *See* Carlton, Peter L.
Mayrand, Marie. *See* Landouceur, Robert.
McCormick, Richard A.
    Pathological Gambling: A Parsimonious Need State Model   258
McDonald, Thomas D. *See* Lindgren, Elaine H.
O'Hara, John.
    "Getting a Stake": Gambling in Early Colonial Australia   41
Puig, Kenneth. *See* Lesieur, Henry R.
Rosecrance, John.
    The Business of Risk by Vicki Abt, James Smith, and Eugene Christiansen   211
Schriner, Eldon C. *See* Lindgren, Elaine H.
Taber, Julian I.
    Compulsive Gambling: An Examination of Relevant Models   219
Tourigny, Yves. *See* Ladouceur, Robert.
Youngs, George A. Jr. *See* Lindgren, Elaine H.

Errata

In Volume 3, issue 1 of the Journal of Gambling Behavior a sex change operation was performed without the author's consent. Mary Dickerson is really Mark Dickerson. We would like to apologize for this error.

THE NATIONAL COUNCIL ON COMPULSIVE GAMBLING, INC.

- was established on December 8, 1972 and incorporated as a voluntary, non-profit agency on May 6, 1975.
- disseminates information and education on compulsive gambling as an illness and public health problem.
- seeks to stimulate the concern of the medical profession, educators, legislators and the criminal justice system on the nationwide problem of gambling and the need for community services and medical treatment for compulsive gamblers and their families.
- proposes a program aimed at the reduction and prevention of compulsive gambling by mobilizing public support through local affiliates and professional groups concerned with the impact of compulsive gambling.
- needs your financial assistance to reach out to families, employees and health professionals by way of press, radio and television.

It will take a major effort to make America aware of compulsive gambling as a public health problem. Donations are tax deductible.

The National Council on Compulsive Gambling, Inc.
444 West 56th Street, Room 3207 S
New York, N.Y. 10019   (212) 765-3833

Membership Application

Name _____

Address _____

City _____ State _____ Zip _____

Telephone: Home _____ Business _____

I want to help you to continue to inform and train on compulsive gambling by joining as a:

Full (voting) Member with 1 year subscription to NCCG Newsletter & 1 year
  Quarterly subscription to Journal of Gambling Behavior .... $ 62
Sponsor .... $ 100
Patron .... $ 500
Institution or Corporation $1000

Check if your corporation will match your contribution _____

Contributions are Tax Deductible   Enclosed is $_____

From HUMAN SCIENCES PRESS

PERIODICALS

PSYCHOLOGY

- **NEW** INTERNATIONAL JOURNAL OF COMPARATIVE PSYCHOLOGY
- **NEW** INTERNATIONAL JOURNAL OF TECHNOLOGY AND AGING
- **NEW** JOURNAL OF BUSINESS AND PSYCHOLOGY
- JOURNAL OF CONTEMPORARY PSYCHOTHERAPY
- JOURNAL OF NONVERBAL BEHAVIOR
- JOURNAL OF PSYCHOLOGY AND JUDAISM
- PASTORAL PSYCHOLOGY
- POPULATION AND ENVIRONMENT
- **NEW** PRE- AND PERI-NATAL PSYCHOLOGY JOURNAL

SAMPLE ISSUES AND COMPLETE PERIODICALS CATALOG
AVAILABLE UPON REQUEST

 HUMAN SCIENCES PRESS, INC. Phone orders: (212) 243-6000
72 FIFTH AVENUE (have credit card information ready)
NEW YORK, N.Y. 10011-8004

From HUMAN SCIENCES PRESS

PARTICIPATIVE SYSTEMS AT WORK
Creating Quality and Employment Security

Sidney P. Rubinstein

"... explains and defends a realistic, operable way to create an integrated mechanism for activating people at all levels of operation to work together for both their own security and the advancement of their company's competitive success."
— Mason E. Wescott
Professor Emeritus
Rochester Institute of Technology

"Participative Systems and Human Sciences Press have done the labor, management and academic communities a real service."
— Stephen I. Schlossberg
Deputy Under Secretary for
Labor Management Relations and
Cooperative Programs
U.S. Department of Labor

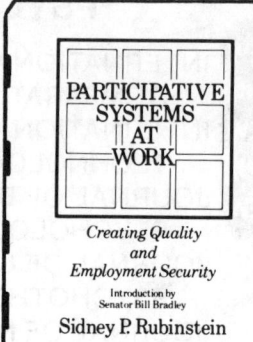

1987
0-89885-338-9 .... 180 pp.
$24.95

Highman, Edith L.
THE ORGANIZATION WOMAN
Building a Career—An Inside Report
Foreword by Sofia Galson
Surveys by Arthur Highman, Ph.D.

In this provocative work on how women get ahead and stay ahead in the corporate world, the perceptions of male and female executives in large U.S. corporations, gleaned from extensive national surveys, are quoted and compared.

"The Organization Woman gathers the perceptions of those women who've made it and the executives to whom they report. It covers a wide range of topics including dealing with superiors and subordinates, understanding organizational culture, making the most of opportunities, and handling specifically sexual issues."
—TRAINING AND DEVELOPMENT JOURNAL

1985   204 pp.
0-89885-237-4 $16.95

ESSENTIAL JOURNALS

CONSULTATION
An International Journal
Editors: Alan Glassman, Ph.D., and Rex Mitchell, Ph.D.

Quarterly Vol. 6 1987   ISSN 0010-3853
Order CONS-D   personal $39.00
Order CONS-F   institutions $87.00

JOURNAL OF CAREER DEVELOPMENT
Editor: Norman C. Gysbers, Ph.D.

Quarterly Vol. 13 1986-87   ISSN 0164-2502
Order JCDE-D   personal $24.00
Order JCDE-F   institutions $65.00

SAMPLE ISSUES AVAILABLE UPON REQUEST

HUMAN SCIENCES PRESS, INC.
72 FIFTH AVENUE
NEW YORK NY 10011 8004

Phone orders: (212) 243-6000
(have credit card information ready)

NEW JOURNAL from HUMAN SCIENCES PRESS

International Journal of POLITICS, CULTURE AND SOCIETY

Edited by Arthur J. Vidich, Stanford M. Lyman and Michael W. Hughey

Published in Association with Florida Atlantic University

This unique interdisciplinary publication provides a forum for discussion, dialogue and debate on points of tension between state and civil society, between nations and global institutions. Its specific problematic is the changing order of public and private spheres of life and the dialectic between rational organization and the emotional needs of human beings. Formerly known as *State, Culture and Society*, the *Journal* encourages historical and analytical essays and article length research monographs.

Issues examined include changing patterns in the coordination of societal and world economic and political institutions; new configurations of ethnic and racial groups and communities; class formations; emergent religions; personal networks and special interests; articulation and social effects of mass culture, propaganda, and the techno-scientific breakthroughs in communication on classical culture and symbolic expression; and the consequences of contemporary social transformations for psyche, self, and kinship.

SAMPLE CONTENTS

Mediterranean and Total Bureaucracies: Some Additions to the Weberian Theory of Bureaucracy by Joseph Bensman; *Class and Religion in American Politics* by Arthur J. Vidich; *Georg Simmel's Sociology of the Sexes* by Heinz-Jürgen Dahme; *Max Weber and the Southwest German School: Remarks on the Genesis of the Concept of the Historical Individual* by Guy Oakes; *Communicative Action or Civilization-Analytic Sociology?: A Critique of Jürgen Habermas' Theory of Reason, Emancipation and the Origins of Modernity* by Donald A. Nielsen; *The Evolving Relationship of History and Sociology* by John Lukacs; *The 'New History' in Sociology* by Gary G. Hamilton; *Nature as News: Science reporting in the New York Times, 1898-1983* by Charles R. Simpson; *Artworks as Symbols in International Politics* by Judith Huggins Balfe; *Public Icons and Bourgeois Novels: Cultural Expression in Francoist Spain* by Aurelio Orensanz; *From Matrimony to Malaise: Men and Women in the American Film, 1930-1980* by Stanford M. Lyman.

Quarterly Vol. 1, 1987-88
Order IJPC-D
Order IJPC-F ....

ISSN 0891-4486
personal $32.00
institutions $75.00

SAMPLE ISSUE OF JOURNALS AND COMPLETE PERIODICALS LIST AVAILABLE UPON REQUEST

HUMAN SCIENCES PRESS, INC.
72 FIFTH AVENUE
NEW YORK, N.Y. 10011-8004

Phone orders: (212) 243-6000
(have credit card information ready)

THE SOCIETY FOR THE STUDY OF GAMBLING

The Society for the Study of Gambling was formed in 1977 to provide a forum for those concerned with research into gambling, to promote its scientific study especially as far as the psychological, social and economic aspects are concerned, and to inform and educate the public about these matters.

The membership of the Society is drawn from a wide circle of people who have an interest in various aspects of gambling. They range from social workers and psychiatrists who deal with 'compulsive gamblers', to members of the gambling industry. It is a condition of the Society that there should be freedom of opinion and practice among its members so that the Society does not take any particular stance in relation to gambling.

The Society holds regular scientific meetings, the proceedings of which are now published in the Society's *Newsletter*.

Issues 1 to 4 of the *Newsletter* include:
Paul Bellringer: Bet you can't win: gambling and the offender.
Iain Brown and George Anderson: Arousal in real and laboratory gambling.
David Dixon: Illegal gambling and histories of policing.
Bill Eadington: Regulatory objectives and the expansion of casino gambling.
Suman Fernando: Alcoholism and gambling: the case of the Jews.
Christopher Hill: The politics of the turf: agenda for research.
David Miers: The provision of credit for gaming.
Gordon Moody: The origins of the Society for the Study of Gambling.
Gordon Moody: Legalized gambling: for or against gamblers?
Ron Pollard: Illegal betting: an industry view.
Howard Rankin: Models of gambling.
Tristram Ricketts: The Horserace Betting Levy Board: its functions and aims.
Also Updates, Correspondence, Notices, etc.

Subscriptions to the *Newsletter* are currently £5 per annum. Up to 3 years are available at the current subscription rate. To obtain all 6 issues already published, remit £9 in addition to subscriptions for 1985 and after. Cheques etc. in favour of the Society for the Study of Gambling should be sent to the Honorable Treasurer: Gerry Taylor, 41 Baginton Road, Coventry, CV3 6JX, United Kingdom.

All other correspondence should be addressed to the Honorable Secretary: Dr. David Miers, Department of Law, University College, Cathays Park, Cardiff, CF1 1XL, United Kingdom.